John Taggart

**The New American Poultry Book**

John Taggart

**The New American Poultry Book**

ISBN/EAN: 9783337813451

Printed in Europe, USA, Canada, Australia, Japan

Cover: Foto ©Thomas Meinert / pixelio.de

More available books at **www.hansebooks.com**

# THE NEW AMERICAN

# POULTRY BOOK,

CONTAINING ALL THE DIFFERENT

## Varieties of Fowls,

WITH COMPLETE INSTRUCTIONS.

HOW TO RAISE POULTRY—THE BEST LAYERS AND SITTERS—
THE BEST SOILS ON WHICH TO KEEP THEM—HOW TO
FEED—MANAGEMENT OF LAYERS AND SITTERS—
POINTS OF BEAUTY——DICTIONARY OF
POULTRY TERMS—INCUBATION—
MANAGEMENT OF THE
MOTHER—
HOW TO REAR THE CHICKS, ETC.

BY

—JOHN TAGGART,—

Bellevue Poultry Farm, Richmond, Pa.

# DOMESTIC POULTRY.

## VARIETIES; THEIR CHOICE AND MANAGEMENT.

In the choice of fowls, no inconsiderable amount of knowledge of the characters of the different varieties is necessary to insure success to the breeder. From my own experience, and that of the most eminent poultry-keepers, I have attempted to jot down such information as may be found useful in the selection and management of these really useful and elegant birds. I shall first introduce to the reader's notice the largest and one of the most important breeds in our country.

## THE BRAHMA FOWLS

Are divided into two classes, the light and dark; as a rule the dark are preferable, although either are good enough for any farm yard. They are now almost universally cultivated throughout America, and a most valuable variety—so hardy, so beautiful, and so excellent in all the relations of poultry life.

The hens are the best of mothers, and lay fine large eggs during the winter. Even when the ground is covered with snow, they lay regularly, and in fact at all times when not employed in sitting or renewing their plumage. The pullets attain full size at an early age, and are in their prime when eight months old.

Brahmas are doubtless the largest of all the varieties of domestic fowls; some have been known to weigh seventeen pounds, which exceeds the weight of any other breed.

LIGHT BRAHMA, COCK AND HEN.

The dark Brahmas have steadily progressed in favor since their first introduction; their gigantic size, great weight, hardihood and prolificacy, and the ease with which they can be kept in confined ranges, all tend to render them much esteemed. To sum up their merits, as good, useful, hardy fowls, they are unsurpassed. They are good layers of good sized eggs, good foragers and good sitters; as mothers they cannot be excelled, no fowls being more careful not to step on their chickens, brooding them better, or searching more diligently for food. The chickens grow fast and are exceedingly hardy; old and young take

good care of themselves, and often recover from ailments that would carry off any of a less hardy sort. They are very good for the table, putting on flesh readily; they are also small eaters.

DARK BRAHMA HEN.

## DESCRIPTION OF THE DARK BRAHMA.

The head of the dark Brahma cock should have a pea comb, that is a triple comb; this should be small, low in front, and firmly set in the head without falling over on either side, distinctly divided, so as to have the appearance of three small combs joined together in the lower part and back, the largest being in the middle, and each part slightly and evenly serrated.

The upper part of the body is silvery white striped with black; the breast, under part of body and thighs either pure black or slightly mottled with white. The feathers that cover the bases of the quill-feathers of the wings are of a lustrous green black, and form a broad well-marked bar across the wings. The flight-feathers are white on the outer and black on the inner webs. The secondary quills have a broad, dark, green black spot at the end of each feather. The tail is black. The shank should be of a yellow color, and well clothed with dark feathers slightly mottled with white.

The hens have a grey head; neck-hackle silvery white, striped with black. The comb is the same only of a smaller size. The remainder of the plumage should be dull white, and closely pencilled with dark steel grey so as almost to cover the ground color and reaching well up the front of the neck. The hen is not so upright in carriage as the cock, and it is much shorter in the legs.

## LIGHT BRAHMAS.

LIGHT BRAHMA HEN.

In color, the light Brahmas are characterized by the general white color of the body, breast and thighs. The neck-hackle should be marked with a distinct black stripe down the centre of each feather; there is a tendency in the cock to come light or cloudy in the hackle—defects which very greatly detract from their beauty. The saddle-feathers in the cock are white or lightly striped with black, those of the hen being white. The first ten flight-feathers are black, but the secondary quills, which alone are visible when the wing is closed, are white on the outer web, consequently the dark color of the wing is not visible when folded. In the cock the tail is black, the tail-coverts being beautifully glossed with green, the lower ones being margined with

LIGHT BRAHMA COCK.

silver, as are the two highest tail-feathers in the hen. The shanks in this variety should be bright yellow, well closed with white feathers slightly mottled with black.

In conclusion I would state that I do not believe, all things considered, that there is any better market fowl than the Brahma; some other breeds are doubtlessly superior table fowls, but they are more tender and harder to rear.

Give your Brahmas large roomy quarters in winter, and if possible plenty of range for exercise; feed well, and they will give you winter-eggs, and those are the kind that bring money.

## COCHINS.

BUFF COCHINS.

The Cochins were first introduced into this country under the name of Shanghaes; they originally come from Shanghae, and are to this day found in great numbers there. But the Shanghaes, as originally introduced and widely grown in this country, were gigantic muscular birds of great activity and wonderful powers of storing away food, which was absorbed into muscle and bone, but made comparatively little juicy flesh. The consequence was, they got a bad reputation, and the term was finally one of reproach; but upon the vast improvement which was made in them by careful breeding, the name of Cochins, as designated by cinnamon or white or buff or partridge, rapidly superseded the old term, and the despised but vastly improved Shanghae sailed under a new name, and are now raised as profitable birds all over the United States.

They are first-class layers, and in season when new-laid eggs are rare, and from their scarcity of so much increased value, this species often proves a source from whence we can obtain supplies. They also make capital mothers, and are quiet when sitting.

In many places where space is limited, the Cochins are found convenient guests; they can put up with worse accommodation, and require less space than almost any other race. I do not mean to say that they will thrive the better for confinement, neither that fowls in general will pine and die if kept in a narrow range; all fowls are better for having ample space; but in cases where their liberties are necessarily abridged and more careful tending is required to counterbalance want of field-room, the Cochin can bear captivity better than any other fowl.

The roosting-poles for Cochins and in fact all bulky fowls should be near the ground; they should be large in diameter in order that the claws may maintain a firm clutch and perfect equilibrium without inconvenience or effort.

## VARIETIES OF THE COCHIN.

The Cochin fowl is a large heavy bird, very broad and clumsy looking. The tail is very short and nearly destitute of feathers, but the remainder of its body is abundantly covered. The legs are short, stout, and well feathered; the head should be small, with a single straight comb; the beak short and strong; the wattles small, and the ear-lobes red and fine as to texture. There are many varieties of the Cochin viz—BUFFS; this is the true type of the colored birds, and for utility, I think the best.

PARTRIDGE COCHINS.—Very heavy; full round plump forms and a majestic carriage.

WHITE COCHINS.—These should be pure white all over. In city yards amid the smoke and dust the White Cochin do not appear to advantage but in the country no variety looks more pleasing, as the beauty of their plumage depends on its clean and unsullied condition.

If well selected, properly taken care of, and well fed, they make a first-class table bird; they are hardy, do not require much space, and I should recommend them to any person who only wants to keep a few birds.

# SPANISH FOWLS.

The Spanish fowls have long been known and highly esteemed in the United States for their great laying and non-sitting propensities.

All fowls are better for being hatched in a warm season, and the Spanish are no exception to this. Though of a sound constitution, no fowl is more injured by cold wet weather. Their

BLACK SPANISH FOWLS.

roosting-places therefore should face the south, and be well-protected from cold winds, especially as they are subject to long and protracted moultings. The cold affects their comb also, which is sometimes frost-bitten, with a liability to mortification.

The flesh of the Spanish Black fowl is juicy and of good flavor, but not equal to that of the "Dorking." The flesh of the White Spanish is not considered so fine in flavor, as that of the Black, yet it is not bad, especially if young.

As layers they are among the best, but are seldom inclined to sit; they generally produce two eggs consecutively and then miss a day.

As to healthiness, they are less liable to roup than lighter-colored birds; in fact, the Spanish fowl is less subject to disease than are most of the common black varieties.

In general they are rather quarrelsome, and are very averse to strange fowls, and if separated from each other even for two or three days, the hens will disagree seriously upon being reunited.

In case of a strange hen being tormented by her companions for any length of time, so that she is afraid to come and feed with them, or of the cock displaying his protracted dislike to her, it will be right to remove her, or she may be reduced to so low a condition as to render her unable to escape their persecutions, and avoid death from their violence.

The Spanish pullets commence laying when six or seven months old, and occasionally sooner, though some of them commence at a later period, according to feeding and treatment. But premature fertility is not to be wished for, as it will frequently happen that pullets which commence very early, seldom lay when fully grown so large an egg as those produce which do not lay before they are eight months old. Indeed the debilitating effects of either premature, or continual laying in ripe age, as respects the Spanish breed are now and then manifested by the loss of the body feathers in moulting, besides the usual falling off of the neck, and wing, and tail feathers; and when thus stripped, the poor birds look very miserable in bad weather.

In sitting Spanish eggs, nine of them are sufficient for hens of ordinary size, as they are much larger than the generality of fowls eggs.

It will be unwise, with any breed, to select the first dozen of a pullet's eggs for hatching; they being comparatively immature and small, it is not likely that large and strong chicks will be the issue. Besides, pullets occasionally do not enter into tender union with their male companions until they have laid five or six eggs.

The color of the Spanish chick, when first hatched, is a shining black, with a blotch of white sometimes on the breast, and a little white also around the bill and the eyes. They do not until nearly grown, get their full feathers, and therefore they should be hatched at a favorable season of the year, to be well feathered before it grows cold in the Fall.

Spanish hens seldom exhibit a disposition to undertake the task of incubation, and if it be attempted, they will in the generality of cases forsake the nest long before the chicks would be hatched. Sometimes, however, they will perseveringly perform the maternal duties; but it is against their general character. They are exceedingly long in the leg, consequently are subject to cramp; this partly accounts for their being so averse to such sedentary occupation. Since, therefore, they will not undertake the office of mothers, we must impose it upon some other class of fowl, that will not only accept the task, but will joyfully hatch and rear the young of even another species until they are able to take care of themselves. It is by this means the Spanish breed is still preserved and multiplied.

## VARIETIES AND DESCRIPTION OF THE SPANISH FOWL.

A full grown black Spanish cock weighs seven pounds; the hen, about six pounds. The principal features, and those which form the most striking contrasts to those of other fowls, are, its complete suit of glossy black, large face, and ear-lobe of white; enlivened by comb and gills of excessive development. The peculiarities of these contrasts induce me to describe them in detail. The plumage is of a rich satin, black, reflecting their shades of bluish, greenish purple, when exposed to the sun's rays; the feathers of the breast, belly, and thighs, are black, of the most decided hue. The hens are of a similar feather, but less brilliant. The face and ear-lobes especially the latter, are of pearly whiteness; the face should extend above the eye, encircle it, and meet the comb; it still increases as the bird grows older, continuing to enlarge in size, especially with hens, which seldom have a really good show of face until two years of age, even beyond the time of their full growth; and the more face and ear-lobe, the more valuable either the cock or hen. The comb of the cock should be erect and serrated, almost extending to the nostrils, and of bright scarlet; it should be fine in texture, and exhibit no sign of excrescences. In hens this uprightness of comb cannot be obtained, owing to its abundant size and thinness of base. The wattles are long, pendulous, of high color, and well folded. The head is long, and there should be no topknot behind the comb, nor muff round the neck. The beak is long, and generally black, it should be slightly curved, and thick at the base. The eyes are very full, bright and of a rich chestnut color: they are somewhat prominent. The neck is rather long, but strong and thick towards the base, the neck hackle being a glossy black; the chest and body are broad and black, the former being particularly dark; the wings are of a moderate size, whilst the coverts are beautifully shaded, and of a bluish black. The thighs are neat but long, as also is the shank, which is of a leaden or dark blue color, and sometimes of a pale blue-white. The soles of the feet are of a dingy flesh-color; the tail is rather erect and well balanced, presenting if well plumed (as it should be) a very elegant green hued shade.

WHITE SPANISH.—These birds are not so hardy, but they inherit the usual qualities of the black; the general feathers, like the face being perfectly white.

THE ANCONA.—There is seldom much white about the face of this variety, and in many cases none; the ear-lobes is, however, of that color, though not so long and full as in the Black. They possess the general characteristics of the Spanish class, and are excellent layers. They are of a very unsettled color, spotted with white but far from regularly marked; they also present many other shades and colors.

MINORCAS.—These are very similar to the last named variety, wanting the white face of the Black tribe; the shank is not so long as in the true Black. They are good layers, but bad sitters and mothers.

ANDALUSIAN.—When carefully selected, the chicks throw black and white and if those most resembling the originals are bred together, a neat grey bird may be obtained. They are good layers, and far better sitters and mothers than the Blacks, and have shorter shanks; whilst their principal peculiarity consists in a tail standing very erect, the feathers of which in many specimens nearly touch the hackle-feathers of the neck. They are a very hardy fowl, and possess a fair share of the Black's good qualities.

There are many other sub-varieties, or rather strains, that have crossed with the Spanish stock, but they neither deserve nor possess a distinct name.

The superiority of the Spanish generally, as egg producers, is so decided, that any cross from them meriting the character of everlasting layers, is worth encouragement. It is to be recollected that the Hamburgh or Dutch is not the only sort from which everlasting layers have sprung. Any hens which with warmth and good feeding will lay eggs continuously, and especially through the winter, are to be welcomed. And though the debilitating effects of continued laying must tell upon the constitution, yet where stock is not desired for a mere gratification of the eye, but kept on economical principles, it cannot be inexpedient to stimulate the prolific powers of hens to the utmost. If good layers which have not the presumption to compete for the prizes of birth or beauty, can by clever management, be induced to lay within two years the entire compliment of eggs which in the ordinary course of nature would not be yielded by them in less than three years, there is an actual saving gained of at least one-third of food, if these effete layers be then fattened and killed. No breed would be better if this plan is strictly applied, than that of the common Blacks of Spanish blood, or some of their sub-varieties.

# THE DORKING FOWL.

Of distinct English breeds the Dorkings are the most celebrated. For those who wish to stock their poultry-yard with fowls of the most desirable shape and size, clothed in rich and variegated plumage, and not expecting perfection are willing to overlook one or two other points, the speckled Dorkings are the breed to be at once selected. The hens, in addition to their gay

DORKING FOWL.    17

GRAY ENGLISH DORKINGS.

colors, have a large vertically flat comb, which, when they are in high health, adds very much to their brilliant appearance. The cocks are magnificent; the most gorgeous hues are frequently lavished upon them, which their great size and peculiarly square-built form displays to great advantage. The breeder, and the farmer's wife, behold with delight their broad breast, the small proportion of offal, and the large quantity of profitable flesh.

The Cockerels may be brought to considerable weight, and the flavor and appearance of the meat are inferior to none. They are only fair layers, but at due and convenient intervals manifest the desire of sitting. Having short, compact legs, they are well formed for incubation. The Dorkings are not well suited for damp soils, by reason of the shortness of their legs. They are also distinguished for breadth of body, the somewhat partridge form, and also, in the poultry phraze, for being clean headed. Though they possess great similarity of form, there is much variety of color; but they are generally distinguished as white, grey or speckled, and also by the character of the comb—viz, as single and double, or rose combed; and classed accordingly at the poultry shows.

The fifth or supernumerary toe is the peculiar mark distinctive of the whole breed under consideration. Though the Creator has not designed anything without its appropriative purpose, this additional member must rather be deemed a distinctive than a useful one, just as the absence of a tail, or the color and size of a comb may distinguish an individual race of fowls. These over-furnished claws have been denounced as sources of danger and annoyance to young chicks when first issuing from the shell, rendering the mother's movements hazardous to them. I have never seen them do so, and even if they did how is the hen to be employed when the sitting fit comes on, for they are persevering sitters, and as neither worrying, nor whipping, nor fettering, nor physicking, or the cold shower bath, will subdue their natural instinct to set, they should be allowed to follow their instinct, and incubate in peace.

The Dorkings are a very heavy fowl when fat, as their frame work is not of that lengthy, incompact structure which it is so difficult to fill up with flesh and fat; they much sooner become tempting figures for trussing and skewering than other fowls. They have a great aptitude for fattening when rendered capons.

## VARIETIES AND DESCRIPTION.

WHITE DORKINGS.—This variety seldom produces more than two broods a year, because they require more favorable seasons, and greater warmth than the colored.

The white is not so large as the colored, and, as a general rule, whiteness in animal physiology is indicative of constitutional delicacy. Their average weight is less than that of the colored, and like all white feathered poultry, the flesh has a tendency to yellowness.

The white cock and hen are perfectly white in the plumage, bills, and legs; both should have a double or rose-comb of bright red, though a single one is frequent, but this is considered a sign of degeneracy. The cock is very upright and spirited in his appearance, and his spurs are usually lower than those in other species. The fifth toe should be well defined. The hen has no individualities.

THE GREY OR SPECKLED DORKING COCK.—The head round, and furnished with double or single comb, of bright red; wattles, large and pendent; the ear-lobes almost white; hackles, a cream white, and the feathers of the hackles dark along the centre; the back, grey of different shades, interspersed with black; saddle feathers, same as hackles in color; wing feathers, white, mixed with black; the larger wing coverts, black; the lesser, brown and yellow, shaded with white; breast and thighs, black or dark brown; tail feathers, very dark, with a metallic lustre.

THE GREY OR COLORED HEN.—Face, lighter colored than that of the cocks; hackles, black and white; back, dark grey; saddle and wing, grey, tipped with black; tail, almost black. Five claws and white legs characterize both sexes.

# POLAND FOWLS.

**WHITE CRESTED BLACK POLISH COCK AND HEN.**

The Polands are excellent layers of perfectly white and moderately-sized eggs, much pointed at the smaller end. They seem to be less inclined to sit than any other breed, and it is judicious to put their eggs under other nurses. The chicks of both sexes, which are hardly distinguishable for many weeks, are very ornamental. The male bird is first distinguished by the tail remaining depressed, awaiting the growth of the sickle feathers, whereas the female carries it uprightly from the first; also, the top-knot in the cockerels hangs more backward than in the pullets.

Their flesh is excellent, being white, tender and juicy.

During three or four years the cocks in particular increase in size, hardihood, and beauty, different in this from fowls generally, which advance much more rapidly to their highest points of perfection, but from which they fall away with corresponding rapidity.

The Polands are extremely tender, and so difficult to rear, that the eggs should not be set before the middle of May, as dampness is fatal to them while very young; but, if they live to be adults, no fowls are more hardy, or profitable as layers, or more delicious for the table. .

Their demerits are few, and of no serious importance. They are not at all suited to dirty farmyards, becoming blind and miserable with dirt. They do not lay quite so early in the year as other tribes, and are not suited for the office of mothers and nurses, from their great disposition to lay; and when they do sit, they are rather unsteady and perverse. Now these objections may be dismissed, because there is nothing to prevent the substitution of hens of other tribes for hatching, and if the Polish hens and pullets themselves in the mean time lay eggs, there is no loss in an economical point of view.

We have good practical authority for stating that the critical period of their lives is from the second to the sixth month.

## DESCRIPTION AND VARIETIES.

The crest of the cock is composed of straight feathers, something like those of a hackle or saddle; they grow from the centre of the crown and fall over outside, forming a circular crest. That of the hen is made up of feathers growing out and turning in at the extremities, till they form a large top-knot, which should in shape resemble a cauliflower. The comb of the cock is peculiar, inasmuch as it is very small, scarcely any on the top of the head, and having in front two small spirals or fleshy horns. The carriage is upright, and the breast more protuberant than in any other fowl, save the Sebright bantam. The body is very round and full, slightly tapering to the tail, which is carried erect, and

22    POLAND FOWL.

which is ample, spreading towards the extremity in the hen, and having well defined sickle feathers in the cock. The legs should be lead color or black, and rather short than otherwise.

POLISH FOWLS.

The varieties among us are the Black; White; the Golden Spangled; and the Silver Spangled.

BLACK POLANDS.—Cock; body, neck, and tail, black, with metallic tints of green; crest, white, with a few black feathers at the base of the bill; comb, very small, consisting **only of two** or three spikes; large wattles, bright red; ear-lobe, white; the skull, instead of being flat as in other varieties, has a fleshy protuberance or round knob.

HEN; the same colors; wattles smaller than those of the cock; in other points the same.

WHITE POLANDS.—These should be pure white all over with the exception of the legs which are of a blue or slate color.

GOLDEN SPANGLED.—Cock; ground color, very bright ochre yellow, black spangles, which, in a particular light, have a beautiful greenish tint; crest, chestnut, with a few white feathers, black beard; comb and wattles small; hackle and saddle feathers, golden yellow; thigh, generally black, but some specimens have them spangled; sickle feathers, dark brown and very large, the smaller side ones lighter in the colors, and beautifully faced with black; legs, slate color.

HENS;—general colors the same; breast, neck, and back, spangled; tail and wing feathers, laced.

SILVER SPANGLED.—The only difference between this variety and the preceding one is in the ground, which is a beautiful silver white.

The Polands very often have crooked backs; when buying them the best mode for detecting the deformity is to lay the palm of the right hand flat on the bird's back, by which any irregularity of either hip, or a curve in the back bone from the hips to the tail will be detected.

# THE SULTAN FOWL.

The Sultans, or Feather-footed White Polish, are a very elegant and pleasing variety, and were imported from Constantinople. They partake of the character of the Polish in their chief characteristics, in compactness of form and good laying qualities.

In general habits they are brisk and happy tempered. They are very good layers of large white eggs, but are non-sitters and small eaters.

As adults they are very hardy, with the exception of the tendency to cold, to which all crested birds are subject when exposed; but the chickens, from their rapid and early feathering, are difficult to rear, evidently suffering severely from the extra strain on their young constitutions.

## DESCRIPTION.

In form they are very plump, full crested, short-legged and compact; the plumage pure and unsullied white throughout and very abundant; their tails are ample, and carried erect; their thighs are short, and furnished with feathers which project beyond the joint, or vulture hocked. Their legs are short, white, and profusely feathered to the feet, which are five toed. The comb consists of two small spikes situated at the base of a full-sized globular Polish crest; the wattles are small and red, wrinkled, both sexes being amply bearded. No fowls are more abundantly decorated—full tail of sickle-feathers, abundant furnishing, boots, vulture-hocks, beards, whiskers, and full round Polish crests, formed of closely-set, silky, arched feathers, not concealing the eyes, but leaving them unobscured.

The legs, as old age approaches, are apt to get red, swollen and inflamed, perhaps from the spur growing in a curved form and producing irritation.

All the varieties of the Polish if kept in a damp situation are liable to a cold, apt to degenerate into roup, and if they are too closely bred, liable to tuberculous diseases and deformity of the spine, causing humpback, they are also very subject to vermin unless supplied with a sand bath; vermin, however, may be readily destroyed by dusting flour of sulpher under the feathers with a common flour-dredger.

# THE MALAY FOWL.

The Malay is a large heavy fowl, with close fitting plumage; it stands very high, and has an upright carriage; height is considered a great point in this breed; the head is small for the size of the bird, with considerable fulness over the eye, which should be pearl, and the hawk bill should be quite free from stain. Like the game fowl, the Malays are most pugnacious and determined fighters, and therefore not suitable for small yards. If they can get no other enemy they will even fight their own shadows.

The chickens fledge late, and have for a long while a bare, wretched appearance. They require a dry, warm temperature, as in youth, before being fully feathered, they are very delicate and highly susceptible of cold and wet.

The Malays are good layers and sitters and after they are full grown, can be kept most anywhere, but on account of their vindictive cruel nature they are by no means desirable to have and my advice is, to have nothing to do with them.

# GAME FOWLS.

BLACK BREASTED RED GAME FOWLS.

This noble race has relationship, though now of remote generations, with the Malays. Before we had any of this breed, the inhabitants of several portions of the Malay or Malacca peninsula, and various parts of the East, possessed them, and used them chiefly for the purpose of cock-fighting.

A thorough-bred Game cock of high degree never fails in courage when opposed to one of his own order. And the Game fowl is the only bird put to the test of combat to prove whether he be genuine or not.

There is a generally recognized standard for form and figure, which must not be departed from, whatever variety of color the birds may present. In weight they vary; four pounds eight or ten ounces was the weight aimed at by the breeders for the cockpit, but six pounds is often reached, when two years old; but beyond this weight impurity of blood may be suspected.

The carriage and form of the Game cock are certainly more beautiful than that of any other variety of domestic fowl. The neck is long, strong and gracefully curved; the hackle short and very close; the breast broad; the back short, broad across the shoulders; the whole body very firm and hard, with a perfectly straight breast and back, the latter tapering toward the tail; the wings large and powerful, and carried closely pressed into the sides; the thighs strong, muscular and short, tightly clothed with feathers, and well set forward on the body, so as to be available for fighting; the shanks rather long, strong but not coarse, covered with fine scales; the feet flat and thin, the toes long and spreading, so as to give a good hold on the ground; the hind toe must be set low down, so as to rest flatly on the ground, and not merely touch with the point—a defect which is known as "duck-footed," and renders the bird unsteady when pushed backward by his opponent.

The plumage is compact, hard and mail-like to a remarkable degree, and possesses a brilliant glossiness that cannot be surpassed. The tail in the cock is rather long, the sickle feathers gracefully arched and carried closely together, the whole tail curved backward and not brought forward over the back—a defect called squirrel-tailed.

The head is extremely beautiful, being thin and long, like that of a greyhound; the beak massive at its root, strong, and well curved; the eye large, very full, and brilliant in lustre; the ear-lobe and face of a bright scarlet, and the comb in undubbed birds single, erect, and thin. The spur, which is exceedingly dense and sharp, should be set low on the leg, increasing its power; spurs are frequently on the hens.

In the hen, the form, making due allowance for the difference

GAME FOWLS.

of sex and alteration of plumage, resembles that of the cock. The head is neater, the face lean and thin. The small thin comb should be low in front, evenly serrated, and perfectly erect,

The deaf-ear and wattles should be small. The neck, from the absence of hackle feathers, looks longer and more slender than that of her mate. The tail feathers should be held closely together, and not spread out like a fan. The plumage should be so close that the form of the wing should be distinctly visible, the outline not being hidden by the feathers of the body.

As the Game fowl is impatient of restraint, a good grass run is essential to keep it in good condition. In breeding great care must be taken in matching, as regards form, feather and the color of the beak and legs. Much depends upon the purity of the hens, for a good Game hen, with a dunghill cock, will breed good fighting birds, but the best Game cock, with a dunghill hen, will not breed a bird good for anything. It is not desirable to mate old birds; a stag, or last year's bird placed with hens two or three years old, will produce finer chickens than when an old cock is mated with last season's hens. For great excellence, four hens with one cock is sufficient.

The hens are good layers and as sitters have no superiors. Quiet on their eggs, regular in coming off, and confident, in their fearlessness, of repelling intruders, they rarely fail to rear good broods, and defend them from violent attacks.

The newly-hatched chickens are very attractive; those of the darker breeds are light brown, with a dark brown stripe down the back and a narrower line over the eye. The duck-wings, grays and blues have proportionally paler hues, but the stripe is seldom absent.

The chickens feather rapidly, and with good care and liberal, varied diet, such as cottage cheese, chopped egg, with a portion of onions, bread crumbs, grits, boiled oatmeal, barley and wheat, with some milk in the earlier stages of their growth, are reared with less difficulty than other fowls.

As Game fowls will fight, and as they are frequently trained for fighting, it is argued that their combs, ear-lobes and wattles should be removed, or "dubbed." This had best be entrusted to the skilled professional.

## VARIETIES.

The recognized varieties of Game fowls are—the Black; Black breasted Red; White; White Pile; Blue; Brown-red; Red Pile; Gray; Spangled; Ginger-red; Silver Duck-wing; Yellow Duck-wing.

DOMINIQUE FOWL.

# THE DOMINIQUE FOWL.

This seems to be a tolerable distinct and permanent variety, about the size of the common Dunghill Fowl. Their name is taken from the island of Dominica, from which they are reported to have been imported. Take all in all, they are one of the very best breeds of fowl which we have; and although they do not come in to laying so young as the Spanish, they are far better sitters and nursers. Their combs are generally double, and the wattles are quite small. Their plumage presents, all over, a sort of greenish appearance, from a peculiar arrangement of blue and white feathers, which is the chief characteristic of the variety; although, in some specimens, the plumage is gray in both cock and hen. They are very hardy, healthy, excellent layers and capital sitters. No fowl have better stood the tests of mixing without deteriorating than the pure Dominique.

SEBRIGHT BANTAM.

# THE BANTAMS.

Bantams are generally kept more for show and amusement than anything else, although, even as profitable poultry they are not destitute of merit; in proportion to the food they consume, they furnish a fair supply of eggs. As table fowls, the hardy little Game Bantams are excellent, plump, full chested and meaty. As useful and ornamental pets, I know of no birds that are superior. The Sebright Bantams are the most esteemed by fanciers. The cocks should not weigh more than twenty-seven ounces; hens about twenty-three, but the lighter in weight the more they are appreciated.

The chicks of the Bantams generally should be hatched in fine weather, and kept for some time in a cozy place.

### VARIETIES.

Golden Sebright; Silver Sebright; Game; Rose-combed Black; Rose-combed White; Japanese; Pekin; Booted White; and White-crested White Polish.

GOLDEN SPANGLED HAMBURG COCK AND HEN.

# THE HAMBURG FOWL.

These fowls are "Everlasting layers" and are seldom inclined to sit. They are too small in size to rear for table, and I think too delicate when young to rear at all; only they are such wonderfully good layers, that one dislikes to dispense with them. They are also known as Chittaprats, Bolton Greys, Pencilled Dutch, Silver Hamburgs, Creole, Bolton Bays, Golden Hamburgs. They are a very noisy fowl, and if the hen-roost should be disturbed at night, nothing but death or liberty will induce them to hold the peace.

SILVER SPANGLED HAMBURGS.

## DESCRIPTION AND VARIETIES.

The Hamburgs have a graceful and upright carriage. The head in the cock is small; beak of a dark color, medium in size; rose comb of a deep red color not inclining to droop on either side, the top covered with small points and ending in a spike; ear-lobes, white of medium size; wattles, red; neck curved; hackle, large and flowing; body, round; breast, very full; plumage close and glossy; legs rather short. The varieties are—Black; White; Golden Pencilled; Silver Pencilled; Golden Spangled; Silver Spangled.

---

# PLYMOUTH ROCKS.

"If there is a better breed for the farmer, or for those who desire both eggs and chickens, we have failed to find it: although many have been tried and 'found wanting.'"

The great popularity that the Plymouth Rock fowl has attained in so short a time, is without a parallel in the annals of gallinaculture, and no other breed is so highly esteemed in America to-day. It has attained this popularity, too, entirely on its own intrinsic merit, without the eclat of foreign origin, or the outlay of large sums of money in "puffing." As *table fowls*, they have no equal in America; being exceedingly sweet, juicy, fine-grained, tender, and delicate. As *spring chickens*, they are the very best breed, for, added to the excellence of their flesh, they feather early, and mature with remarkable rapidity. As *market fowls*, they are unsurpassed, being large (cocks weigh 9 to 11 pounds, hens 7 to 9), and very plump bod:es, with full breasts, clean, bright yellow legs, and yellow skin; they always command the highest price. As *egg-producers*, they are only excelled by the Leghorn class, and lay more eggs than any other breed that

## PLYMOUTH ROCKS.

hatches and rears its own young, and can be depended upon for eggs all the year round. Their eggs are also of large size, very rich,

and fine-flavored, from white to redish-brown in color. In hardiness, both as chicks and mature fowls, they are also unequaled, and being out-and-out an American breed, they adapt themselves to all climates and situations better than any other breed. Their combs and wattles being of moderate size, are not liable to freeze, and they have no feathers on the lower part of their legs to drabble in the snow and mud, and thereby chill them. In plumage, they are bluish-gray, each feather distinctly penciled across with bars of a darker color, hence are very admirable, and not likely to become soiled by the smoke and dust of the city. Added to their fine plumage, their symmetrical form and upright and pleasing carriage enable them to vie with most breeds, either upon the lawn, in the yard of the fancier, or in the exhibition hall. As mothers, they are excellent, being neither non-sitters nor persistent sitters, are kind and gentle, and good foragers. In disposition, they are quiet, gentle, and cheerful, bear confinement well, and are easily confined, their wings being too small, and bodies too large to admit to much progress in flight. If given range, they will find their own living, and if confined, need a remarkably small amount of food for such large fowls. In fine, this comparatively new breed combines all the sturdy and excellent qualities of the ideal fowl to a wonderful degree, (the merits of the large flesh-producing and small egg-producing breeds,) filling a place long sought for, but never before attained, and is a golden mean. It is pre-eminently the farmer's and mechanics' fowl—in fact the BEST fowl for all who have facilities for keeping but one variety, and desire that one to be a "general purpose" breed.

# LANGSHANS.

LANGSHAN FOWL.

The Langshan is the latest acquisition to our poultry yards from Asia, and, judging from our experience with other Asiatic breeds, their origin certainly augers well for their future in this country. They are natives of northern China, and consequently accustomed to its rugged climate.

The discoverer of this variety in China was a scientist in the employ of the British government, and not a "chicken fancier," particularly. Eight years ago, he wrote thus to his English friends: "I send you some fine fowls by the steamer *Archilles*, of Hall & Holt's line. They are clear black, and are called *Langshans*. Look out for their arrival and send for them without delay." \* \* \* A second letter stated that "the fowls I am sending you are very fine. Their plumage is of a bright glossy black. I have never seen any like them before, and I am told their flesh is excellent. The Chinese say they are allied to the wild turkey; they are very valuable birds. You must be very careful of them, and get them acclimated by degrees."

These birds we sent to Major A. C. Croad, Durington Worthing, England, from his nephew, who was, a few years ago, upon an exploring expedition under orders from the English government, in the north of China, where he discovered this fine variety of fowls, in the province of *Langshan*, and sent home the first that were ever seen in England.

Upon the arrival of the *Archilles*, in England, Major Croad lost no time in sending for his birds; and the messenger, on his return, informed him that the new arrivals had received quite an ovation in the docks, people crowding to have a look at them, asking what breed they were, and whether they were for sale, etc. The captain of the steamer told him that, although he had been several times to china, he had never met with any fowls like these before.

The Langshans were publicly exhibited the next year at the Crystal Palace and other leading shows, and were bred successfully for three or four years, the stock being kept under the supervision of the agents of the original importer.

They were of late years imported to America, and our American fanciers speak well of them; in fact they are the best birds that were ever imported from China. Langshans have straight red combs, somewhat larger than those of Cochins. Their breast is full, broad and round, and carried well forward, being well meated, similar to the Dorkings. Their body is round and deep like the Brahmas. The universal color of the plumage is a rich metallic black. The tail is long, full feathered, and of the same color as the body. The color of their legs is a blue black, with a purplish tint between the toes. The average weight of a cockerel, at seven or eight months, when fattened, is about ten pounds; and a pullet about eight pounds. Their carriage is stylish and stately.

The good qualities claimed for the Langshans are the following: They are hardy, withstanding readily even severest weather. They attain maturity quite as early as any of the large breeds. They lay large, rich eggs all the year round, and are not inveterate sitters. Being of large size, with white flesh and skin, they make an excellent table fowl; more especially so on account of the delicacy of the flavor which the flesh possesses. To briefly summarize, I may then say that this breed is worth the attention of all. Firstly, because they come from a part of the world which has given us many of our most excellent breeds; and secondly, because their popularity is in the ascendency, and they seem to combine in themselves nearly all the valuable characteristics that go to make up a practically useful fowl.

I give in connection with this article a wood-cut of a pair of Langshans, believing that a faithful illustration will do more to give an accurate idea than even an extended description. It will be observed that, apparently, they are more like the Black Cochin than any other breed with which we are familiar, but in reality they differ very essentially from them.

# WYANDOTTES.

This new breed have so many points to recommend them, both to the fancier and farmer, that they will surely become very popular. Their plumage is white, heavily laced with black, the tail alone being solid black; the lacing on the breast is peculiarly handsome. They have a small rose comb, close-

THE WYANDOTTES.

fitting; face and ear lobes bright red. Their legs are free from feathers and are of a rich yellow color. In shape they bear more resemblance to the Dorkings than any other breed. Hens weigh 8 to 9 pounds, cocks 9 to 10 pounds, when full grown. They are very hardy, mature early, and are ready to market at any age. Their flesh is very fine flavored and close grained, which, with their yellow skin, model shape and fine, plump appearance, particularly adapts them for market. They are extraordinary layers, surprising every breeder at the quantity of eggs they produce. If allowed to sit they make most careful mothers, are content anywhere, and will not attempt to fly over a fence four feet high. Their great beauty and good qualities will make for them a host of friends wherever the breed is introduced.

# THE LEGHORN FOWL.

ROSE COMB BROWN LEGHORN.

This abmirable breed of fowls has become widely disseminated in the United States. They are valued for their many good qualities, among which are beauty and constant laying propensities.

BROWN LEGHORN COCK.

They are very hardy fowls, possessing all the advantages of the Spanish without their drawbacks. Their legs are bright yellow, and perfectly free from feathering on the shanks. The faces are red, the ear lobes only being white. The comb in the cock is thin, erect and evenly serrated. In the hen it falls over like that of a Spanish hen. The tail in the cock is exceedingly well furnished with side sickle-feathers, and in both sexes is carried perfectly erect. The birds are active, good foragers, and have a very handsome and sprightly carriage. They are abundant layers of full sized eggs, the hens rarely showing any inclination to sit, but laying the whole year round, except during the annual month. The chickens are very hardy; they feather quickly and mature rapidly, thus having the advantage over the Spanish.

BROWN LEGHORN HEN.

These fowls are exceedingly useful as well as ornamental addition to our stock of poultry; they are more valuable to egg-farmers than breeders of table fowls, as they are but small eaters and so do not put on flesh quickly. To people, however, who depend on their poultry bringing them a constant supply of eggs, they are invaluable.

## LEGHORN VARIETIES.

Black; White; Brown, and Dominiques.

LEGHORN FOWL.

# THE FRENCH BREEDS.

CREVECŒURS.—These birds are generally supposed to be of Norman origin, and to owe their name to the little village of Crevecœurs, not far from Lisieux. They are fine, well plumaged black birds, with large crests on their heads, in the front of which are situated the two horns, or spikes, which arise from the bifurcation of the comb. They give the bird a very curious look, and make his head resemble the pictures of that of his Satanic majesty. The birds are well shaped, with rather large legs of a leaden grey color. The hens lay large white eggs, but are not good sitters. The pullets mature early, and as they lay soon, put on fat readily, and are of a good shape for table; they are, in dry warm localities, profitable fowls to keep; they bear confinement well, but are rather difficult to rear, and have a decided tendency to "roup.,' If crossed with Brahmas or Leghorns they might probably become more hardy.

## LA FLECHE FOWLS.

These birds may be considered, I think, the best of the French fowls for table; they are also more hardy than the Crevecœurs, and have more size and more style, being handsome, upstanding birds, in color jet black, with rich, metallic plumage; their ear lobes are large and perfectly white, their faces bright red and free from feathers. The comb in good well-bred birds does not vary with the sex, and is in the shape of a pair of straight horns; the leg-scales are lead color, hard and firm. The cocks are tall without being at all leggy; the hens have large and rather long bodies, longish necks, and thin clean legs. The best specimens come from the North of France, though they are not even there easy to procure, as the French do not go in for keeping the different breeds of fowls distinct, so it is hard to obtain really pure-bred birds.

## HOUDANS.

HOUDAN COCK AND HEN.

These are considered the best French fowls, and of late years have become great favorites with poultry-fanciers. They have, like the Dorkings, five claws on each foot; their plumage is black and white, shaded with violet and green; they are crested birds, the crest turning backwards over the neck; their cheeks are well feathered, and wattles well developed. They differ from other species by several remarkable traits, the head forms a very obtuse angle with the neck, so that the beak is depressed and viewed from above appears like a nose. The flat square comb looks like a fleshy forehead; the cheeks are surrounded with curling feathers which resemble whiskers; the reversed corners of the beak have the appearance of a mouth. The crest looks like a head of hair, and the entire visage instantly reminds the spectator of a man's face.

Houdans are hardy, not difficult to rear good steady layers, but non-sitters; they put on fat readily, and are very good table fowls, flesh excellent and shapely in form.

## THE DOMESTIC TURKEY.

DOMESTIC TURKEY.

The domestic turkey can scarcely be said to be divided, like the common fowl, into distinct breeds; although there is considerable variation in color, as well as in size. The finest and strongest birds are those of a bronzed-black; these are not only reared the most easily, but are generally the largest, and fatten the most rapidly. Some turkeys are of a coppery tint, some of a delicate fawn-color, while others are parti-colored, grey, and white, and some few of a pure snow white. All of the latter are regarded as inferior to the black, their color indicating something like degeneracy of constitution.

To describe the domestic turkey is superfluous; the voice of the male; the changing colors of the skin of the head and neck; his proud strut, with expanded tail and lowered wings, jarring on the ground; his irascibility, which is readily excited by red or scarlet colors, are points with which all who dwell in the country are conversant.

The adult turkey, is extremely hardy, and bears the rigors of winter with impunity even in the open air; for during the severest weather, flocks will frequently roost at night upon the roof of a barn, or the branches of tall trees, preferring such an accommodation to an indoor roost. The impatience of restraint and restlessness of the turkey, render it unfit company for fowls in their domitory; in fact the fowl house is altogether an improper place for these large birds, which require open sheds and high perches, and altogether as much freedom as is consistent with their safety.

Although, turkeys will roost even during the winter months on trees, it is by no means recommended that this should be allowed, as the feet of these birds are apt to become frostbitten from such exposure to the air on the sudden decline of the temperature far below the freezing point.

Turkeys are fond of wandering about pastures, and the borders of fields, or in fact any place where they can find insects, snails, slugs, etc., which they greedily devour. In the morning, they should have a good supply of grain, and after their rerurn from their peregrinations another feed; by this plan, not only will the due return home of the flock be insured, but the birds will be kept in good condition, and ready at any time to be put upon fattening diet. Never let them be in poor condition—this is an axiom in the treatment of all poultry—it is difficult, and takes a long time, to bring a bird into proper condition, which has been previously poorly fed or half starved.

The turkey hen is a steady sitter; nothing will induce her to leave the nest; indeed, she often requires to be removed to her food, so overpowering is her instinctive affection; she must be freely supplied with water within her reach; should she lay any eggs after she has commenced incubation, these should be removed—it is proper, therefore, to mark those which were given to her to sit upon. The hen should now on no account, be rashly disturbed; no one except the person to whom she is accustomed, and from whom she receives her food, should be allowed to go near her, and the eggs, unless circumstances imperatively require it, should not be meddled with.

The hen usually sits twice in the year, after laying from a dozen to fifteen or more eggs, on alternate days, or two days in succession, with the interval of one day afterwards, before each breeding. She commences her first laying in March; and if a second early laying is desired, after she has hatched her brood, it is economical to transfer the chicks immediately after they leave the shell to another turkey-hen which had begun to incubate contemporaneously with her, and will now take willing charge of the two young families. This, however, cannot be viewed as a benevolent proceeding; and much less so if the mother be deprived of her offspring, and the consequent pleasure of rearing them, for the purpose of putting a fresh set of eggs under her, which she will steadily hatch for three or four weeks more. In this case, however, fowls' eggs are usually given, from merciful consideration to abridge the period of incubation from thirty-one to twenty-one days.

According to the size of the hen, the season, and the range local temperature, the number of eggs for each hatch may be stated at from eleven to seventeen; thirteen is a fair average number. As the hen lays them, her eggs should be immediately removed, and kept apart until the time for sitting them; else the awkward bird might break them in the nest, as she goes in or out of it. While she is incubating, the cock bird should not be permitted to approach it, lest he should mischievously break the eggs or disturb the hen.

On about the thirtieth day, the chicks leave the eggs; the little ones for some hours will be in no hurry to eat; but when they do begin, supply them constantly and abundantly with chopped eggs, shreds of meat and fat, curd, boiled rice, mixed with lettuce, and the green of onions. Melted mutton suet poured over barley or Indian-meal dough, and cut up when cold is an excellent thing. Little turkeys do not like their food to be minced much smaller than they can swallow it; indolently preferring to make a meal at three or four mouthfuls to troubling themselves with the incessant pecking and scratching in which chickens so much delight. But at any rate, the quantity consumed costs but little; the attention to supply it is everything.

As in the case of young fowls, the turkey chicks do not require food for several hours after they have emerged from their shells.

It is useless to cram them as some do, fearing lest they should starve; and besides, the beak is as yet so tender that it runs a chance of being injured by the process. There is no occasion for alarm if, for thirty hours, they content themselves with the warmth of their parent and enjoy her care. When the chicks feel an inclination for food, it will soon become apparent to you by their actions, then feed them as I have before directed.

## FATTENING.

About the middle of September or the first of October, it will be time to begin to think of fattening some of the earliest broods, in order to supply the markets. A hen will be four or five weeks in fatting; a large cock two months or longer, in reaching his full weight. The best diet is barley or Indian meal, mixed with water, given in troughs that have a flat board over them, to keep dirt from falling in. A turnip with the leaves attached, or a hearted cabbage, may now and then be thrown down to amuse them. When they have arrived at the desired degree of fatness, those which are not wanted for immediate use must have no more food given them than is just sufficient to keep them in that state; otherwise the flesh will become red and inflamed, and of course less palatable and wholesome. But with the very best management, after having attained their acme of fattening, they will frequently descend again, and that so quickly, and without apparent cause, as to become quite thin. Turkeys fatten faster, and with less expense, by caponizing them, which, also, produces better and sweeter flesh.

## THE GUINEA FOWL.

THE GUINEA FOWL.

Of all known birds, this, perhaps is the most prolific of eggs. Week after week and month after month see little or no intermission of the daily deposit. Even the process of moulting is sometimes insufficient to draw off the nutriment the creature takes to make feathers instead of eggs. From their great aptitude for laying, and also from the very little disposition they show to sit, it is believed, that these birds in their native country, (Africa) do not sit at all on their eggs, but leave them to be hatched by the sun.

It is not every one who knows a cock from a hen of this species. An unerring rule is, that the hen alone uses the call note "come back," "come back," accenting the second syllable strongly. The cock has only the harsh shrill cry of alarm, which, however, is also common to the female.

There is one circumstance, in regard to the habits of the guinea cock, that is, he pairs only with his mate in most cases, like a partridge or a pigeon. In the case where a guinea cock and two hens are kept, it will be found, on close observation, that though the three keep together so as to form one pack, yet that the cock and one hen will be unkind and stingy to the other unfortunate female, keep her at a certain distance, merely suffering her society. The neglected hen will lay eggs, in appearance, like those of the other, in the same nest. If they are to be eaten, all well and good; but if a brood is wanted and the eggs of the despised one chance to be taken for the purpose of hatching, the result is disappointment and addled eggs.

It is best to hatch the eggs of the guinea fowl under a hen of some other species; a Bantam hen makes a first class mother, being lighter, and less likely to injure the eggs by treading on them than a full sized fowl. She will well cover nine eggs, and incubation will last about a month.

Feed the chicks frequently, five or six times a day is not too often, they have such extraordinary powers of digestion, and their growth is so rapid, that they require food every two hours. A check once received can never be recovered. In such cases they do not mope and pine, for a day or two, like young turkeys under similar circumstances and then die; but in half an hour after, being in apparent health, they fall on their backs, give a convulsive kick or two, and fall victims to starvation. Hard-boiled egg, chopped fine, small worms, bread crumbs, chopped meat, or suet, whatever, in short, is most nutritious, is their most appropriate food.

# THE DOMESTIC GOOSE.

THE DOMESTIC GOOSE.

With respect to the range and accommodation of geese, they require a house apart from other fowls, and a green pasture, with a convenient pond or stream of water attached. The house must be situated in a dry place, for geese at all times, are fond of a clean, dry place to sleep in, however much they may like to swim in water. It is not a good method to keep geese with other poultry; for when confined in the poultry-yard, they become very pugnacious, and will very much harrass the hens and turkeys.

In allowing geese to range at large, it is well to know that they are very destructive to all garden and farm crops, as well as to young trees, and must, therefore, be carefully excluded from orchards and cultivated fields. It is usual to prevent them getting through the gaps in fences, by hanging a stick or "yoke" across their breast.

Those who breed geese, generally assign one gander to four or five females. When well fed, in a mild climate, geese will lay twice or three times a year, from five to twelve eggs each time, and some more, that is, when they are left to their own way; but if the eggs be carefully removed as soon as laid, they may be made, by abundant feeding, to lay from twenty to fifty eggs without intermitting. They begin to lay early in the spring, usually in March, and it may be known when an individual is about to lay, by her carrying about straws to form her nest with; but, sometimes, she will only throw them about.

When a goose is observed to keep her nest longer than usual, after laying an egg, it is a pretty sure indication that she is desirous of sitting. The nest for hatching should be made of clean straw, lined with hay, and from fourteen to eighteen eggs will be as many as a large goose can conveniently cover. She sits about one month, and requires to have food and water placed near her, that she may not be so long absent as to allow the eggs to cool. The most economical way of getting a great number of goslings, is to employ turkey hens to hatch, and keeping the goose well fed she will continue laying.

Goslings must be kept from cold and rain as much as possible. Feed them on barley or Indian meal or crusts of bread soaked in milk.

## VARIETIES.

African; Toulouse; Embden; Egyptian; White Chinese; Brown Chinese.

# THE DUCK.

MUSCOVY DUCK.

It is not in all situations that Ducks can be kept with advantage; they require water much more, even, than the goose; they are no grazers, yet they are hearty feeders. Nothing comes amiss to them in the way of food: green vegatables; kitchen scraps; meal of all sorts made into a paste; grains; bread; worms; insects; all are accepted with eagerness. Their appetite is not at all fastidious; in fact they eat most everything, and eat all they can. They never need cramming, give them enough, and they will cram themselves; but remember, confinement will not do for them; they must have room, and plenty of it, also a large pond or stream, if you have these requirements they can be kept at little expense.

Where they have much extent of water or shrubbery to roam over, they should be looked after and driven home at night, and provided with proper houses or pens; otherwise they are liable to lay and sit abroad. As they usually lay either at night, or very early in the morning, it is a good way to secure their eggs, to confine them during the period when they must lay, a circumstance easily ascertained by feeling the vent.

COMMON DUCK.

The duck is not naturally disposed to incubate, but in order to induce her to do so, you may, towards the end of the laying, leave two or three eggs in the nest, taking care every morning to take away the oldest laid, that they may not be spoiled. When she shows a desire to sit, from eight to ten eggs may be given according to the size of the duck, and her ability to cover them. The duck requires some care when she sits; for as she cannot go to her food, attention must be paid to place it before her; and she will be content with it, whatever be its quality; it has been remarked that when ducks are too well fed, they will not sit well. The period of incubation is about thirty days.

WILD DUCK.

The duck is apt to let her eggs get cold, when she hatches and many thereby are lost, this together with the fact of her often leading the ducklings into the water immediately after they are excluded from the shell and thus losing many if the weather is cold, often induces poultry keepers to have duck eggs hatched by hens or turkey hens; and being more assiduous than ducks, these borrowed mothers take an affection for the young, to watch over, which requires great attention because as these are unable to accompany them on the water, for which they show the greatest propensity as soon as they are excluded, they follow the mother hen on dry land, and get a little hardy before they are allowed to take to the water without any guide.

The best mode of rearing ducklings depends very much upon the situation in which they are hatched. For the first month, the confinement of their mother, under a coop is better than too much liberty. All kinds of sopped food, buckwheat flour, Indian or barley meal and water mixed thin, worms, &c., suit them.

When ducklings have been hatched under a common hen, or a turkey hen and have at last been allowed to go into the water, it is necessary, to prevent accidents, to take care that such ducklings come regularly home every evening; but precautions must be taken before they are permitted to mingle with the old ducks lest the latter ill-treat and kill them, though ducks are by no means so pugnacious and jealous of new-comers as common fowls uniformly are.

## VARIETIES.

ROUEN DUCKS.—The flesh is abundant and of good flavor; good specimens will dress from five to seven pounds each.

AYLESBURY DUCKS.— These are considered the most valuable of the English breeds and is well thought of in this country. They are good layers, but do not weigh quite as much as the Rouen breed.

CAYUGA DUCKS—These are the finest of the American breeds, they are also the largest and most valuable of the duck family. They weigh generally from eight to ten pounds, are good layers, and easily raised.

The other varieties are the Mandarin; Carolina; Muscovy; Call Duck; Black East India.

The duck is peculiarly the poor man's bird (its hardihood renders it so entirely independant of that care which fowls perpetually require); and indeed of all those classes of persons in humble life, who have sloppy offal of some sort left from their meals, and who do not keep a pig to consume it. Ducks are the best save-waste for them; even the refuse of potatoes, or any other vegetables will satisfy a duck, which thankfully accepts, and with a degree of good virtue which it is pleasant to contemplate, swallows whatever is presented to it, and very rarely occasions trouble. Though fowls must be provided with a roof and a decent habitation, and supplied with corn, which is costly, the cottage garden waste, and the snails and slugs which are generated there, with the kitchen scraps and offal, furnish the hardy ducks with the means of subsistence. And at night they require no better lodgings than a nook in an open shed; if a house be expressly made for them, it need not necessarily be more than a few feet in height, nor of better materials than rough boards and clay mortar, a door being useless, unless to secure them from thieves.

## POINTS OF POULTRY.

*A*—Neck hackle. *B*—Saddle hackle. *C*—Tail. *D*—Breast. *E*—Upper Wing coverts. *F*—Lower Wing coverts. *G*—Primary quills. *H*—Thighs. *I*—Legs. *K*—Comb. *L*—Wattles. *M*—Ear-lobe.

## Dictionary of Poultry Terms.

BEARD.—A bunch of feathers under the throat of some breeds, as Houdans or Polish.

BREED.—Any variety of fowl presenting distinct characteristics.

BROOD.—The number of birds hatched at once; a family of young chickens.

BROODY.—When the hen desires to sit she is said to be broody.

CARRIAGE.—The upright attitude or bearing of a fowl.

CARUNCULATED.—Having a fleshy excrescence or protuberances, as on the neck of a turkey-cock.

CHICK.—A very young fowl.

CHICKEN.—A name applied to fowls until they are full grown.

CLUTCH.—The eggs placed under a sitting hen, also the brood hatched therefrom.

COCKEREL.—A young cock.

COCK.—The full grown male bird.

COMB.—The crest or red fleshy tuft growing on top of a fowl's head.

CREST.—A top-knot of feathers, as on the head of the Polands.

CROP.—The first stomach of a fowl, through which the food must pass before the process of digestion begins.

DEAF-EARS.—Folds of skin hanging from the true ears, varying in color.

DUBBING.—To cut off the comb, wattles, &c., leaving the head smooth.

EAR-LOBES.—Folds of skin hanging from the ears.

FACE.—The bare skin extending from the top of the bill around the eyes.

FLIGHT-FEATHERS.—The primary wing feathers, used in flying.

FLUFFS.—The downy feathers around the thighs.

GILLS.—A term sometimes applied to the wattles; the flap that hangs below the beak.

HACKLES.—The peculiar narrow feathers on a fowl's neck.

HEN-FEATHERED.—A cock, which owing to the absence of sickle feathers resembles a hen.

HENNY.—The same as hen-feathered.

HOCK.—The elbow joint of the leg.

KEEL.—The breast bone.

LEG.—The shank.

LEG-FEATHERS.—Feathers growing on the outside of the shank.

MOSSY.—Uncertain marking.

PEA-COMB.—A tripple comb.

PENCILING.—Small stripes running over a feather.

POULT.—A young turkey.

PRIMARIES.—The same as flight-feathers.

PULLET.—A young hen.

ROOSTER.—A word used in the United States to designate the male fowl; generally called cock.

SADDLE.—The posterior of the back, the feathers that cover it are termed saddle-feathers.

SECONDARIES.—The quill-feathers of the wing, which show when the fowl is at rest.

SHANK.—The leg.

SICKLE-FEATHERS.—The upward curving feathers of a cock's tail.

SPANGLED —Spots on each feather of a different color from that of the ground color of the feather.

SPUR.—A sharp bone protruding from the heel of a cock.

STRAIN.—A race of fowls that has been bred for years unmixed with other breeds.

TAIL-COVERTS.—The curved feathers at the sides of the bottom of the tail.

TAIL-FEATHERS.—The straight feathers of the tail.

THIGHS.—The upper part of the shanks.

TOP-KNOT.—The same meaning as crest.

TRIO.—One cock and two hens.

VULTURE-HOCK.—Stiff projecting feathers at the hock-joint.

WATTLES.—The red fleshy excrescence that grows under the throat of a cock or a turkey.

WING-BAR.—A dark line across the middle of the wing.

WING-COVERTS.—The feathers covering the roots of the secondary quills.

# POULTRY-KEEPING.

Any person who takes up poultry-keeping should have *some end* in view; should either keep fowls for showing and prize-taking, or for laying and fattening. Fowls for domestic use and fowls for exhibition are two totally different things, and call for entirely different methods of treatment.

In this small book I wish to adhere as much as possible to the business of poultry-keeping on *a small scale* within the means of all people living in the country, and having a little ground of their own.

If there is a farm-yard to fall back on, and the birds are not kept by themselves, but are allowed to run with the other inmates of that yard, having a hen-house in which to roost, lay, and sit, then your cares are reduced to a minimum. As all who might and should keep poultry, have, however, no farm, but only a garden and a plot of ground, I will not say any more about the old farmyard system, but suppose that the fowls have to be kept on a small scale without the foregoing advantages. Much depends on the purpose for which fowls are kept, if for show and prize-taking, or merely for domestic uses, for table and for eggs.

If for show, then the different breeds must be kept thoroughly pure, entirely distinct, and great attention given to points generally. A higher class of fowl must be purchased in the first instance; the diet must be more generous, size being a great point with judges; and the whole business of poultry-keeping is placed on a more costly footing, and becomes an expensive and but rarely a remunerative amusement; whereas in merely keeping a small stock of fowls for table use—the first and original outlay of purchase and house-building overcome—you should, and can easily, have, with a little trouble, a small profit each month after the necessary food is paid for.

I have done both myself: kept fowls for general use—ordinary common birds, mostly cross-bred—and kept purely-bred birds to show, and I have no hesitation in saying that the former is the best plan, unless, of course, you are a poultry fancier and have money enough to allow you to indulge your mania for prize birds; then, with highly-bred stock, you may look to the sale of eggs and the taking of prizes to, in a measure, recoup you for your outlay. I was fairly successful with the high-class birds I purchased, and got good prices for the sitting of eggs I sold, as also for the birds themselves when I parted with them; but I cannot honestly say I consider the keeping up of select and distinct sorts is worth the trouble it entails—that is, if you do the work of looking after them yourself. Mine, I know—I could not afford to keep a poultry-man — led me a sad dance. I was always in trouble with them; they had separate houses and runs, but unless I was near while the different sorts were having their outing there was sure to be some disturbance, a fight between the cocks through the bars and netting, and this very likely occurred just before I wanted to show one of them, when featherless heads and wounded bleeding combs would be the result; and the hens too were nearly as pugilistic. Some one will probably remark, "Mismanagement." Possibly; but I had not all the proper arrangements a regular prize poultry-breeder would have, and even in the very best regulated poultry-yards accidents will, we know, occur, and so these creatures were a perpetual torment to me.

And when, after an interval of some years, I began poultry-keeping again, I started on an entirely different plan and on a very small scale. It is from my experience then gained that I offer the following hints to those living in the country who wish to keep poultry and yet do not mean to incur much expense in so doing.

For general use I would say do not keep entirely to pure-bred birds, but mix them with others; a good cross-breed is often more desirable than a really pure breed; not only are the fowls resulting from the cross stronger and less likely to become sickly and degenerate, but you can, by a judicious selection in the cross you allow, counteract many of the qualities you do not consider quite desirable.

## BEST BREEDS FOR MARKET.

I do not believe there are any better market fowl, all things considered than the Langshans, next comes the Brahmas. The Dorkings are a superior table fowl, but are tender and hard to rear.

## EGG PRODUCERS.

The Black Spanish; Polands; Houdans and Hamburgs are all inveterate layers; but the Black Spanish and Hamburgs are rather tender, and more fit for the fancier than for the practical man. For a desirable "all round" breed, I should recommend the Plymouth Rocks. At any rate I have described the different breeds, given you their good and bad points, and you may take your choice.

## SORTS FOR SMALL YARDS.

If you have only a limited space to allow for your birds, do not keep too many at first. Possibly, as you find your poultry answer, you may wish to considerably increase your stock, and so will have to enlarge your premises, which by that time you may be able to do; besides, you will have gained experience during the time you have been looking after a limited number, and will have learned many things respecting the nature of fowls, their habits, diseases, constitutions, and general characteristics, of which before you were entirely ignorant.

My own opinion is, I own, entirely against a very large poultry-farm. I should always prefer having a small one under my own immediate eye to possessing a quantity of birds and being obliged to keep a man or woman to look after them.

If people *want to lose money by poultry* let them mass them in numbers, and they will soon gain the desired result. If, on the contrary, they will be content with modest profits, and patiently turn over pennies instead of expecting to turn over dollars, then let them keep poultry on a small scale, attend to them themselevs, spare no pains or trouble in looking after and thoroughly understanding the requirements of their stock, and they need not fear but that the result will be satisfactory.

To buy pens, nests, rent land, pay a man to look after the stock, waste money in sundries and expensive food, buy useless items, and hand over all trouble to subordinates, *is not the way to make poultry pay.*

While, on the other hand, to look after a little poultry-yard yourself, to vary the food by economising all kitchen refuse, buying up cargo rice and second-class grain—which is really quite good enough for fowls, and better suited to them than very good barley, oats, or wheat—never to allow food to be wasted, nor to keep an old and useless stock, *is the way to insure certain small profits*, if those will content you.

In trying to grasp too much you stand a chance of losing even more than the original outlay. A great many people, who have now little plots of ground suitable for fowls, but standing empty, are deterred from keeping poultry by the idea that it is so expensive a proceeding, and that they will eventually be out of pocket by it. So they will, certainly, if they commence on too large a scale; but if they began with a dozen or two dozen fowls, and and kept the original stock down to that number, only allowing the chickens for killing during the season, and pullets for laying to swell the numbers each year, then we should hear less about poultry expenses, and more about eggs and chickens.

Now with regard to commencing operations. BRAHMAS, LEGHORNS, PLYMOUTH ROCKS and LANGSHANS are the fowls I should keep. Brahmas as winter layers, good sitters, and good mothers; Plymouth Rocks as good all round, and Langshans are especially for table.

The number of hens I would allow to each cock would be; Leghorns, twelve hens to each cock; Brahmas, eight hens to one cock; Plymouth Rocks, six hens to one cock; Langshans, six hens to one cock.

## THE FIRST OUTLAY.

If you have an adaptable outhouse, which can, with a little contrivance and a little money spent on it, be turned into a fowlhouse, you are indeed lucky, for you will then for a few dollars, say fifteen at the outside, be able to fit it with perches and nests, and see to the flooring, roofing and ventilation.

Your nests, of strong wickerwork or straw, will not cost you more than 25 cents each. You should have twelve at first. You can easily have more if you want them for sitting purposes, but you certainly will not require a nest for each hen. An old saucepan for cooking the food your kitchen will probably supply. Your water-pans should be of common strong yellow stoneware.

If you have no run, you must inclose one with wire, and this will be rather expensive; but your fowls, if they are to be kept in a certain degree of confinement, must have exercise, so a run or yard is an *absolute necessity.*

You should have a door in the run, at one of the ends adjoining the house, and a door besides in the house itself, with an opening in it, closed by a slide, for the fowls to go in and out as they like.

In the run must be the sheltered place for the dust-bath and for the birds to run under in case of rain. (*See* "Houses and

Yards.") This inclosure I should not have covered at the top.

The height of three rows of wire, one on top of the other—*i. e.*, 72 inches—will be quite high enough to prevent heavy birds getting out over; and the Hamburghs, who are by nature great roamers, must have their wings clipped; it will not improve their appearance, but, as they are not kept for showing, that will not much matter. The wire netting you will be able to fix yourself with a little help, unless you are lone women in the house, in which case you will have to get some man who is clever at doing odds and ends of work to help you.

*It is a fatal error to cramp fowls.* Better far to have a small healthy family of poultry than a large sickly one. If a few birds are well looked after and made comfortable they will be more likely to pay than a number badly kept and allowed too little room.

If from want of space or want of money you can only keep a few fowls, do not be discouraged. A cock and a couple or three or four hens will not eat much, but on the principle of "every little helps" the eggs and two or three broods of chickens from them in the year will be something; they will give you amusement in looking after them, and if you do not sell but merely eat the eggs and the chickens, they will help out the household bills and pay for the extra food you will require; for with only three or four birds, household scraps, if carefully economised, and a little grain daily, will be quite enough to keep them healthy.

There are a great number of poultry-books, and very excellent ones too; but most of them are written with the object of instructing would-be poultry-keepers in the method of keeping a large number of fowls, but few hints being given to people who can only afford to keep a few, and those not for exhibition and show, but really for use. It is, however just these small poultry-keepers we want to see multiplied in America, for until poultry-keeping becomes a national industry—which it cannot unless taken up by the million—so long will the money which should be kept in the country be sent out of it for eggs and chickens, more particularly for the former articles.

Poultry-farming on a large scale has been tried often in America, of late years more especially, but hitherto it has not proved very successful; it does not do so, though, in other countries. When fowls are massed they become unhealthy; this has been proved very frequently. It is not poultry-farming on an extensive plan, however, that I advocate, but *general fowl-keeping*. I would wish to see every laborer with his few fowls, making a little extra money by the eggs and chickens they produce. To do this, however, profitably there must be *thrift*, and in this valuable quality I fear the Americans as a nation are found wanting. Our cooking is by no means good or economical; this is a well-known fact. Where a French peasant's wife will set her husband down to appetising food, be it only a tasty *potage*, an American mechanic's wife will put before hers ill-cooked food costing far more, but less nourishing from the fact of its being so badly dressed. Here is a decided want of *thrift*. So in poultry-keeping, peasants in France keep a cock and a few hens as a matter of course, but feed them very economically on household and garden scraps, various odds and ends, and so make them not only pay their way, but help in the housekeeping besides. Unfortunately we as a nation do not care to trouble over small matters, or attend to the merest details, as the French do; yet it is just this attention to trifles which makes poultry-keeping on a small scale pay.

It is far better to attend to everything yourself—in fact, unless you have plenty of money and can have an experienced man or woman to look after your stock, you must do so. Leave nothing undone for the comfort of your birds, and go through your daily work in your poultry-yard regularly and methodically.

## HOUSES AND YARDS.

If you have to build a fowl-house it need not be in any way an expensive erection. Let it be, if possible, built on to an outside wall of the house, say with its back to the kitchen or greenhouse, in such a position as to insure some degree of warmth to the inmates. Let the floor be dry, the roof weather-tight, and the ventilation good, and your fowls will be sure to do well in it. The cheapest material to make it of would be *rough boards*. The roof can also be boarded, only in that case it should be covered with felt. The holes for ventilation should be so placed that the birds feel no cold air on them while roosting. Such a house should measure at least eight feet square, and the roof should slope from about seven to five feet. The door should lock, and a trap-door should be made in it for the hens to go in and out at will: this trap-door should be a sliding one, and easily closed when required, at night being always kept shut for fear of foxes, cats, &c.

*Perches* should be round poles, not less than four or five inches in diameter, and should not be set too high up—an error into which many people fall. Three feet from the ground is quite high enough for the most elevated perch, and there should be others lower, two and a half feet and two feet from the ground

If perches are too high, heavy fowls cannot fly up to them with ease, and in descending are certain in time to injure themselves, bending or breaking the breastbone and injuring their feet.

*The floor* should not be of brick, stone, or wood, but of beaten earth well battened down until it presents a perfectly smooth, hard surface, which should be swept out carefully daily and sanded or sprinkled with fine sifted ashes. If, however, you have to build a house for your birds, there being no outhouse you can turn into a fowl-house, then you might prepare a floor of either chalk battened down until quite hard, the ground being dug out to the depth of a foot and filled in with the chalk, over which should be spread sifted ashes or sand; or else fill in the space dug out with burnt clay, also thoroughly rammed down and spread over with a wet mass of cinders, fine gravel, quicklime, and water; this when dry forms a very good floor.

*The nests* should be arranged so that they are screened from view and darkened, not placed high up for the same reason as before given with regard to the perches, and they should have a ledge in front of them for the hen to step on before going into her nest or on leaving it, else in flying down eggs are frequently dragged out and broken in the fall; and if chickens are hatched high up they are liable to creep out of the nest, fall down, and die. Soft straw is the best lining for nests, as it does not harbor insects so much as hay. It should be *frequently changed* unless hens are sitting, and then it is best not to disturb the hen, or she may forsake her nest. Nest-eggs of stone or china are easily procured, and should be kept. Many hens will not lay in a nest unless there is an egg already in it, and will forsake a nest they have been laying in if all the eggs are removed. Some people leave in the nest an ordinary egg, but this plan is most objectionable; it imparts to the nest a musty smell, and gives also a taste of *must* to those fresh eggs which are laid in it, and which, though really fresh in themselves, have thus a disagreeable odor and taste, quite leading one to suppose that they were stale. This is the reason why so many eggs brought to table have this defect; people will not take the trouble to change the straw in the nest often enough. Besides all this there is the danger of the stale nest egg breaking, which if it does, the nest, and even the whole hen-house, will become offensive. A stone nest-egg can always be kept in a nest, and if a hen wants to sit, a few placed under her form a good trial of her steady sitting powers, and settle her on her nest before the real eggs she has to hatch out are placed under her.

If you keep more than one sort of fowl you must have divisions in your houses. If it is built either against the kitchen wall, or back to some room in which there is in winter constantly a fire, the effect of the warmth will be apparent in the greater number of eggs your hens will lay during the cold weather. Or the hen-house could be built on to a greenhouse wall which is kept heated in the winter. The nests should be resting against the warm back wall, and the birds roosting on the perches will also feel the benefit of the heat. It is astonishing how much fowls enjoy warmth. This is the reason why cottager's fowls lay often very much earlier than those kept by amateurs, because they are generally kept in a lean-to outhouse built against the cottage wall close to the fireplace. The fowls by this means get the warmth of the fire, and in some cases they actually roost in the kitchen. All poultry-keepers could have their fowl-houses run up outside some fireplace or flue, which would keep the birds warm without the expense of an extra fire.

*Yard or Run.*—If fowls are not allowed free range, which is not always possible on account of gardens or neighbors, a space should be inclosed for them, either fenced off with wooden pailings or wire netting. In this run should be a plot of grass, and if possible a shrub or two for the birds to pick insects off. If the space allows of it there should be a small covered shed in one corner for the fowls to run under during the rain, as fowls cannot endure damp, and under this shed should be the *dust-bath.* It is a downright necessity for all birds to roll or *bathe* in the dust.

They are very particular about their toilets. This may sound to some absurd, but it is most important. No fowls will keep in health unless they are clean, and by rolling in fine dust and ashes, and covering themselves with them, they clean themselves and get rid of the fleas and parasites with which they are always more or less infested. Fowls that are allowed their entire freedom always make dust-heaps for themselves, and retire to them daily.

If it is possible to have a little running stream conducted through this yard then you may indeed consider yourself fortunate, but most likely you will have to content yourself with pots and pans for water. Let these be shallow, and change the water frequently. The question of coops for chickens I have considered in the chapter on Hatching, but I may mention here that the shed in the yard would be a very good place for mother hen and her family when the weather was damp. A shed need not be an expensive building. A few rough poles, with a felt roof, could be easily made by any one, and it is a very great boon to fowls. It need not be of any great size or height, only the roof should have a considerable slope for the rain to run off.

# FOOD.

Overfeeding is as great a mistake as underfeeding. Three times a day is quite enough to feed old fowls: a good meal in the early morning, another before going to roost, and a midday feed. Many people, however, only feed twice; this, if the fowls have a farmyard to dig and forage about in, is enough, but in limited space I should certainly feed three times, giving grain for the last meal as more sustaining and stimulating. Chickens, of course, require food much more frequently.

Before I describe the various sorts of food suitable for poultry, a few general directions will be advisable.

*Feed regularly*—that is, at stated hours—and do not get into the habit of giving handfuls of grain in and out in the course of the day; if you do so you will spoil the birds' digestion.

A supply of pure fresh water is another absolute necessity. Every day in winter the pans should be washed out and filled with fresh water, twice a day in summer if the weather is very hot.

All poultry like *a change of diet*, and should on no account be fed day after day with the same food; as fowls are not fastidious, but will eat nearly any food, there is no possible reason why a variety of food should not be given them, and it is certain they will thrive and do better when their tastes are consulted a little.

*Rice* is a cheap food, but is not very nutritious, therefore should be given mixed with other foods; it may, however, be considered as an excellent food for fowls which are not kept up for show purposes, and if poultry are suffering at all from diarrhœa should be at once given instead of their ordinary food. Rice, whenever given, should be *cooked* as the raw grain is most injurious, and by swelling in the crop after it has been swallowed often makes the fowl "crop-bound." It should be prepared thus:—Boiled until the grains are completely separated, not in hard lumps, but easy for the birds to pick up when scattered about in the yard; a piece of dripping dissolved in the water in which the rice is boiled has a wonderfully softening effect on it. In winter I always mix a little coarse black pepper with the cooked rice. Fowls in cold weather need stimulants; and pepper, when given in sparing quantities, is very good for them. Rice can often be purchased very cheaply; many grocers sell what they term "fowl-rice," but if you are tolerably near a seaport you can very often get the chance of buying damaged "cargo" rice, which, though possibly just a little injured by seawater, is still excellent food for poultry. I have ranked rice first because of its cheapness. Of the different sorts of corn *barley* is the least expensive, but it is too heating to feed fowls on it alone; it should be ground into meal, mixed with water and fine bran or scraps, and given in a crumbly state, not too moist nor yet too lumpy.

Cooked or prepared food is good for all live stock of all descriptions, for experience proves it to be more nutritious from the changes effected, and therefore more readily digested. One writer advises the following mixture:—

One peck of fine middlings and half a peck of barley-meal placed in a coarse earthenware pan and baked for one hour, then boiled water is poured in and the whole stirred together until it becomes a crumbly mass—or the baked middlings can be mixed with rice, previously boiled—two meals of this mixture might be given each day, and one meal of grain.

*Oats* are good for laying hens, but to my mind are best ground; it is not at first a favorite food with poultry, but they soon acquire the taste, and it is even more nourishing than barley, but also more expensive. Oatmeal is considered wonderfully good and fattening diet, and in Ireland is generally used for poultry— that is, when they are kept up for market, the meal is mixed with milk and mashed potatoes. In oats there is as great an amount of starch as in barley, more flesh-forming substance, and more fat-producing matter.

*Light Wheat* is the grain I prefer for poultry-food; but, alas! it is not easy to procure, though it is cheap as far as price goes. If you have a farmer living near you he may perhaps let you have some as a favor; but, as a rule, farmers keep it for feeding their own poultry, and do not care to sell it at all.

*Buckwheat and Hempseed* are very good, the latter to be given during moulting, but they are too expensive to be given frequently.

*Indian Corn* is good and economical food, but too fattening to be used much; as a change, though, it is desirable; its usual cheapness, compared with the price of our home-grown grains, commends it in some places; it should not however, be given whole, but ground into meal and mixed with water or milk.

*Linseed* is chiefly given to prize fowls and those intended for exhibition; it increases the secretion of oil, and makes their plumage shine and look glossy.

*Potatoes* steamed and mashed are very nourishing, but rather expensive.

*Bullock's Liver* boiled and cut up into small pieces may be given with much advantage once or twice a week to birds kept in small inclosures.

*Malt* is one of the best things for poultry, but not very easy to procure; if, however, you are near a brewery you will not have so much difficulty in obtaining it. It induces early and continued laying; should be given sparingly, either bruised or whole, about two handfuls for every six fowls; it can be mixed with the ordinary food. For chickens also it is desirable, about one handful to every six; if they are fledging it assists them in putting on feathers, and at all times helps their growth.

*Milk* should be constantly given—that is, where a cow or cows are kept, otherwise perhaps it would be rather an expensive addition to the cost of poultry-keeping; but if the food is wetted with fresh milk, or a little warm milk stirred into the rice or various meals in use, it is astonishing how very much further the food goes, for it gives a satisfying property to it, and is most nourishing, especially for the younger members of your fowl family.

*Green foods* are all good, and should be given daily: chopped cabbage, clover-heads, turnip-tops, lettuce, turnips, boiled or steamed, form also a good change of diet, and grass fresh cut from lawns, or a handful plucked and thrown into the yard now and then, will be much appreciated. Fowls, as I said before, are by no means fastidious in their tastes; grain, soft, animal, and green foods all come alike to them; worms, maggots, and slugs are also delicacies, but not very often procurable, though French poultry-keepers and others take the trouble to form heaps of earth, manure, dead leaves, and so on, on purpose to generate supplies of worms with which to feed their fowls.

To those who would keep fowls economically, and yet profitably, I say save *all* table and house scraps. If you do not keep a pig you will have plenty for the fowls: crusts of bread, stale pieces, scraps of meat, fish, vegetables, bones broken up, soup bones, after they have been used and their goodness extracted by boiling down for stock, yet contain no small share of nourishment; broken and pounded till small, they are almost necessities for fowls kept in partial confinement.

If you feed fowls on grains and expensive meals you cannot expect a profit from them; but if, on the contrary, you utilize house-scraps—which would otherwise be wasted—and give green food, you will be a considerable gainer; if you have to buy all the food, of course you will find poultry-keeping rather an expensive amusement instead of a paying one.

My poultry family I feed in this fashion—that is, the stock birds—the chickens, of course, have more delicate food, and that more frequently given:—

*First meal*, given about 7 a. m.—fowls are early risers—is of grain, inferior barley, or wheat-tailings, or meal in a crumbly state.

*Second meal*, midday, of soft food, pickings, such as bread, sops, meat and fish scraps, with either barley, oats, or Indian meal mixed with it, or else boiled rice, peppered in winter.

*Third meal*, before going to roost, grain. I vary the food as much as possible, sometimes giving two meals of grain and one of soft food, at other times two meals of soft mixture and one of grain, and at least once a week give chopped liver, well boiled but fresh—not in the horrible putrid state some people suggest. I could not fancy eating a fowl fed on carrion myself, though I know it is frequently done; but the flesh on fowls so fed must, one would naturally think, be gross and rank-tasting.

*Water* should be plentifully supplied fresh and pure and the pans refilled frequently in summer; in winter all water-pans should be emptied out at night, as, if the water freezes in them they often crack or break.

*Lime and mortar rubbish or broken oyster shells* should be freely scattered about the yards, also gravel and small stones. Fowls like to pick such things up; besides, it is necessary that they eat some shell-forming material or their eggs will be soft, which is very often the case if such substances are not provided. I do not believe in cooking or grinding *all* the grain foods, and should certainly give wheat-tailings or inferior small barley in its natural state. If the birds could not digest it they would not have been provided by Nature with an elaborate apparatus for softening and grinding it. If we feed entirely on moist food even fowls in confinement, we must weaken the action of the gizzard by not giving it enough work to do. The two extremes of feeding entirely on cooked and moistened food, or entirely on grain or hard food, are both mistakes; vary the food, and allow only one meal of solid grain, which should be given either as the *first* or *last* meal, but do not so completely interfere with Nature's laws, as to weaken an organ which is purposely provided to render the natural food wholesome. By allowing plenty of lime and mortar rubbish in your yards, small stones, and so on, your fowls, even in confinement, will be able to digest a small portion of grain each day. I am well aware that many poultry-fanciers say *cook all food*, but I am certain that too much moistened food is not altogether good. I can only speak from my own experience, and I never found the creatures under my care suffer from eating small whole uncooked grain once a day.

The gizzard is a most powerful grinding-mill, being composed of very thick muscles, and lined with a tough insensible coriaceous membrane. The two largest muscles which form the grinding apparatus are placed opposite each other, face to face, just like two millstones, and they working on each other grind to a pulp the food which is subjected to their action and break it down until it is in a fit state to be acted upon by the gastric juice, which softens the grain. Until, however, it has gone through Nature's grinding-mill the gastric juices have no power upon it to render it solvent. By giving food constantly which does not require the action of this apparatus upon it to render it wholesome we run the risk of injuring it by inaction : this surely stands to reason. In the case of chickens even a little very small grain should be given, that while the gizzard is growing it may have something to act upon, and no grain is so good for this purpose as the tailings of wheat before-mentioned.

It is a bad practice to underfeed poultry, or, in fact, any young stock; but, on the contrary, do not waste food; scatter it for them, and when they cease to run after it stop feeding them, is a fairly good rule to go by. It is said that one full-grown bird will eat half-a-pint of grain each day, because, though it may not positively consume that amount of grain—what with meal-scraps, green stuff, &c.—it consumes food to about that value.

# INCUBATION.

Of artificial incubation I may as well say at once I have had no experience; therefore it is a subject of which I do not presume to write; but I cannot think that it is at all adapted to very small poultry-yards, for it must entail primary outlay, endless trouble and considerable expense. On large farms it may answer, or with persons who are bitten with the poultry mania, love trying everything new that they hear of, and have more money than they know what to do with unless they indulge in some hobby or hobbies to help them in making away with it. The invention of the artificial incubator cannot be considered, however, as a new invention, for as early as 1848 Mr. Cantelo, manager of the Model Poultry Farm at Chiswick, brought out the "Cantelonian Hydro-Incubator," and shortly afterwards Mr. Rouillier invented another—an improvement on the one named. Since then their name has been Legion.

The old natural method of allowing the hen to sit on her eggs and hatch out her small family is the only plan of which I have had practical experience, and as being an entirely natural process I cannot but think it the best, especially for poultry-keepers on a small scale.

There are very many little matters connected with eggs, and hatching them out, which can only be learnt by much practice and long experience of domestic fowls, their manners and habits.

This can only be gained by being constantly with them and carefully watching them through all the various stages of their lives.

It is never very difficult to procure a broody hen. Your Brahma hens will most likely be quite willing to sit, probably more often than you wish them to. Be careful, however, not to put under her at once the eggs which you have selected for your sitting. She should be moved in at night, placed on a sitting of china eggs, and allowed to sit on them for at least two days before you entrust her with real eggs.

Now about the eggs themselves. Probably you have, out of your family of hens, some that are better than the others, either in shape and form, or more handsomely marked, or better layers, or there is something or other about them, some distinguishing point, which leads you to wish to perpetuate their stock. Their eggs should, therefore, be saved; but do not keep eggs certainly beyond a fortnight; the fresher the eggs the better, I believe. Those you set apart for a sitting remove directly they are laid and place them in bran, small end downwards, dating them in ink, and adding the name of the hen. Does this sound absurd? Possibly to people who know little and care less about fowls it may, but those who keep a limited number I venture to say would have their original family of birds named, either by names caused by some distinguishing mark about the bird, or in groups adhering to one initial letter.

When you have collected, say, thirteen eggs, which is quite enough to put under any hen, though people do advise fifteen for a large hen—too many really for a hen, though a turkey would cover them comfortably—thirteen for a large Brahma hen, and eleven for a smaller hen are the number I usually place under the hen, and find them quite enough. If a nest is too full of eggs there is sure to be an accident: some eggs get broken and the nest gets foul and sickly; besides, the hen covers a compact nest of eggs much better, and they all get an equal share of heat.

All the eggs placed under the hen should be marked with their proper dates. Have the eggs as near as possible in date, so that the chicks may hatch out close together. A great advantage of marking the eggs is, that should the hen lay any when first beginning to sit, or should other hens gain access to the nest, the fresh eggs laid can be removed. Mr. James Long, a great authority on poultry, advises that at the end of ten days the eggs should be tested. This should be done in the evening by the light of a lamp, holding the egg betwixt the thumb and forefinger of the right hand in front of the flame, and shading the large end with the base of the left hand, the air-chamber is discovered; this is apparently opaque, the rest of the egg being dark and heavy, the two portions being divided by a clear black line—that is, if the egg is fertile. If, on the other hand, the egg is light and opaque throughout, or, in other words, exactly like a new-laid egg when held before the same light, it is not fertile. This little test is so simple that every one should adopt it, and use the eggs found unfertile, not returning them to the nest. They are just as edible and as wholesome as eggs laid on the same day but not placed under a hen, and can always be used in the kitchen, being quite as good if not better than the so-called "cooking eggs." Sometimes, however, these unfertile eggs are not clear and edible, but rotten; this can generally be detected. If the egg, on being tested in the manner described, is found neither clean nor fertile with the dark line at the top, but without the dark line and dull throughout, especially in the centre, the whole mass within the shell being in a movable state, its condition may be reasonably suspected and it can be thrown away. This state may arise from one or more causes; it is fancied that it arises from the fertilization being incomplete or weak, wanting sufficient strength to break into positive life, but yet enough to affect the rest of the egg, which, as in all cases in which any life has existed, decomposes, and in time engenders gas. Such eggs should be buried, not thrown where they can be picked at by other birds.

It is a good plan to sit two or more hens at the same time; on the tenth day you can test the eggs, and remove from both nests the unfertile ones giving one hen all the other eggs and resitting the other on a fresh lot of eggs. Besides, if two hens sit at once, one hen when they hatch out can take both broods, so you economise your stock of hens. I would never advise, as some people do, that hen No. 2 should be given a fresh set of eggs and have to sit another three weeks, for no hen could sit six weeks without taxing her strength too much; this proceeding I look upon as a downright cruel one.

Short-legged hens are the best for sitting, therefore Brahmas and Dorkings make very good "broody" hens. Three weeks is the usual time it takes for hens' eggs to hatch, but they may either be a day or two before or a day or two after the twenty-one days.

If possible have a sitting-house, or arrange that your sitting hens are kept in a quiet, rather dark place, away from the other birds, else you will have endless trouble; for if kept in the same house in which the other hens lay, they will be constantly interfering with the sitting hens, trying to lay in the same nests, and eggs are sure to be broken in the scuffle. Your sitter may prove a little restless in a fresh place at first, but employ china eggs for her to sit on until she is disposed to sit steadily, and she will soon settle down, you will find, in her new nest, especially if she be really "broody" or "cluck." And here it may be as well, perhaps, to say a few words about "broody" hens. Sometimes they are most tiresome, and very often this strong desire to sit, which is termed *storge*, is so strong that no means you can try will abate it. In such a case I should be tempted, even if I did not want the chickens, to let the poor hen gratify her desire, and do as the French *acoureurs* do. They only provide broods, but do not *rear them*, selling their chickens at twenty-four hours old, and sending them to the *fermiere* who has ordered them packed up warmly in flannel in a small flat basket. Chickens, curiously enough, travel very well at that early age, better even than when they are older, because Nature provides them with nourishment when they first hatch out, and they really need nothing till the next day but to be kept snug and warm. When they reach their destination, which must, of course, be within reasonable distance, they are given at night to a hen who has a brood of chickens of about the same age, who will, as a rule, welcome the addition to her family with pleasure, seeming rather to delight in this mysterious increase to her family. A hen is always very proud of a large brood, and I have often noticed will apparently, in hen language, crow over a less fortunate mother with only a few to take care of.

I once had a hen who had only one chick. She got shut away from her nest by accident, and was kept out so long that the eggs were spoiled all but three, and from these were hatched very weakly chicks. Two died in the act of being liberated from their shells, and the result of the sitting of thirteen eggs was one chick, and that took a considerable amount of cosseting and nursing before it became quite strong. It was most absurd to see the mother, the fuss she made over her one bantling. It was a late sitting, and I had no other chicks ready to enlarge her family. When the chick was a few days old, her favorite mode of carrying it was on her back, and there the little creature sat quite contentedly while the hen marched about. This went on for months, until really the single scion of the house of "Raca" was as strong as his mother. But the affection between the two was too funny. Even when he was a fine handsome cockerel, about to be promoted to reign in the room of his father "Raca" as Raca II., or over another harem, his mother would insist on presenting him with scraps and dainties she had picked up. I never knew a case in which the tie of relationship betwixt hen and chick lasted so long.

To return to the subject of "broody" hens. I certainly wonder why here in America we do not adopt French methods with regard to rearing poultry. We spend days, weeks, in trying to cure a hen of wishing to sit, a perfectly natural inclination, very often starving and really cruelly teasing the poor thing, while all that time she might be fulfilling her end in life, and sitting on a nest full of eggs. She does not cost more while she is sitting, and, indeed, it is far more economical to employ her than to chase the poor wretch off the nests, shut her up, give her physic, or otherwise torment her. You may argue, "Oh, but my hen would lay again soon if I prevented her from sitting!" Pardon me, but the hen certainly would *not* lay under a month, and probably not for six weeks, as she will pine at first and lose flesh from the feverish anxiety of her state, will be some time before she gets in condition again, and very often two or three months will elapse before she will lay; whereas, after sitting, even if her chickens are removed from her or she is only left with one—perhaps you feel inclined to allow her one or two after her trouble of sitting so long—she will begin to lay again sooner than she would were she laboring under the *storge*. If it is very late in the season you might get ducks' eggs and sit your "broody" hen on them. Ducks do better in cold, inclement weather than chickens, and when sold bring in a good price. They cost more to fat, though, as they are such ravenous feeders.

Sitting hens should have a *daily* run. Do not remove them forcibly from their nests, but let the door be open every day at a certain hour for a certain time while you are about. Perhaps for the first day or two you may have to take them gently off their nests and deposit them on the ground outside the door. They will soon, however, learn the habit, and come out when the door is open, eat, drink, have a dust-bath, and return to their nests. That this should be a daily performance is quite necessary to their health and well-being. It is a very old and mistaken notion to fancy that the chicks hatch out better if the hen sits close and never leaves her nest, because it is not so; air, food, exercise, and a roll in the dust are necessary to the hen's health, and the eggs will not come to any harm.

Some people, while hens are off their nests, damp the eggs with lukewarm water. Moisture, they say, is necessary, and the chicks gain strength by the process. This may be correct, and, in very dry weather, perhaps necessary. Myself I never fancied it did much good, though I have tried the experiment; but I consider it is a mistake to meddle too much with nest or eggs; the hen is only made restless and dissatisfied by so doing, and the result is not such a very decidedly good one as to be worth the extra trouble. While the eggs are hatching out do not touch the nests; it is very foolish to fuss the old bird and make her angry, as she treads on the eggs in her fury, and crushes the chicks when they are in the most delicate state of hatching—*i. e.*, when they are half in and half out of the shell, when a heavy tread on the part of the old bird is nearly certain to kill them.

Picking off the shell to help the imprisoned chick is always a more or less hazardous proceeding, and should never be had recourse to unless the egg has been what is termed "billed" for a long time, in which case the chick is probably a weakly one and may need a little help, which must be given with the greatest caution, in order that the tender membranes of the skin shall not be lacerated. A little help should be given at a time, every two or three hours; but if any blood is perceived stop at once, as it is a proof that the chick is not quite ready to be liberated. If, on the contrary, the minute bloodvessels which are spread all over the interior of the shell are bloodless, then you may be sure the chick is in some way stuck to the shell by its feathers, or is too weakly to get out of its prison-house.

The old egg shells should be removed from under the hen, but do not take away her chicks from her one by one as they hatch out, as is very often advised, for it only makes her very uneasy, and the natural warmth of her body is far better for them at that stage than artificial heat.

Should only a few chicks have been hatched out of the sitting, and the other remaining eggs show no signs of life when examined, no sounds of the little birds inside, then the water test should be tried. Get a basin of warm water, not really hot, and put those eggs about which you do not feel certain into it. If they contain the chicks they will float on top, if they move or dance the chicks are alive, but if they float without movement the inmates will most likely be dead. If they (the eggs) are rotten they will sink to the bottom. Put the floating ones back under the hen, and if, on carefully breaking the others, you find the test is correct (one puncture will be sufficient to tell you this), bury them at once.

Chickens should never be set free from their shells in a hurry, because it is necessary for their well-being that they should have taken in all the yolk, for that serves them for food for twenty-four hours after they see the light, so no apprehension need be felt if they do not eat during that period, if they seem quite strong, gain their feet, and their little downy plumage spreads out and dries properly. Their best place is under the hen for the time named, then they may be fed in the manner described under the head of "Management of Chickens."

## MANAGEMENT OF CHICKENS.

Chickens will, as I have already said, do without food for the first day and night; but as soon as they begin to feed they should be very well fed, and constantly. We all know the old saying, that "Children and chicken are always picking." At first their food should be crumbs of bread, sometimes dry, sometimes soaked in milk, and the yolk of hard-boiled eggs crumbled up and mixed with bread-crumbs. This is quite enough for the first week. Afterwards small grain may be given, chicken wheat, or tailings of wheat, groats, canary-seed, a very little hempseed, bits of underdone meat minced small, a little finely-chopped green food, macaroni boiled in milk and cut into small bits, and so on. They should be fed very often, but only given a little at a time. I feed mine every two hours for the first three weeks or so, taking care that they only have just as much as they can eat at a time, so that the food is not wasted. Hempseed must be given with caution; but if the weather is cold and damp it is very good for warming the chicks, and they are very fond of it. Soft food mixed dry should be given them after the first week, macaroni, barley-meal, or middlings. This mixture should be made with milk, or, if no milk is given, then scalded water, but on no account should any food for chickens be mixed with water which has not been *boiled or scalded*. The food should not be mixed in a wet, sloppy mass, but of such a consistency that when thrown on the ground it will crumble readily.

The old hen should be supplied with grain (wheat), some of the meal, or any other food suitable for her when her little ones are fed, but not oats. All water which is given to the chickens should be boiled first, or else it is very apt to give them diarrhœa. A very good drinking-pan can be made for the small birds by inverting an ordinary flowerpot in its saucer, and filling the latter with water. In this they cannot drown themselves, as they might in a deeper pan or ordinary drinking-trough. Many people give skim-milk instead of water at first.

All the time chickens are growing they should be well fed. It is the very greatest mistake to stint any young stock; and chickens, if you wish to bring them on quickly for market, must be well and generously fed at all ages, not neglected when three-parts grown, as is too often done. They should be constantly supplied with fresh water.

It is certainly best to confine the hen under a coop for the first month or so. If she is allowed her liberty she will wander about with her brood in search of insects, and so may expose her family to the attacks of hawks, weasels, or other vermin. And, besides this, though you wish to feed your hen well while with her brood, it would be rather foolish to allow her to satisfy her appetite on the dainties prepared for them, which she naturally will do unless you give them their meal where she cannot reach it, but giving her under her coop at the same time coarser food. Economy points out that delicate and expensive food, such as groats, boiled eggs, and crumbs of bread, should be reserved for the chicks, while the hen has wheat or ordinary food. I should not feel inclined to give her oats or barley unbruised for this reason: she will, of course, call her little ones joyfully to her to partake of the food given her, and they might choke themselves with large whole grain, such as oats or barley. Rice will not hurt them (boiled, of course), nor wheat, which is a much smaller grain, especially in tailings, than the other cereals mentioned, and cannot injure her little family, even if she does give them a grain or two.

For the first week or two the coop should be placed in a warm sheltered spot, but taken into a safe place at night. As the chicks gain strength it should be moved on to a grass plat. The ordinary-shaped coop, with a sloping roof and barred front, is as good a one as any, only I should advise handles, strong wooden ones, being fixed to each side to facilitate movement. Boarded bottomed coops are not desirable—it is far better to place a bottomless coop on the ground—else you might have small wheels to your coops to push them along when changing their place. In a case of emergency, or if the expense of a coop cannot be incurred, an old cask or beer-barrel makes a very fair coop. Knock out one end and put laths across, leaving one to draw in or out, and take out the staves which rest on the ground. The barrel should be propped on each side to prevent its moving, and a tarpaulin must be provided to throw over it at night to prevent any rain soaking in the knocked-out end, and will serve as a cover for the opening, which must be closed, for fear of cats, foxes, rats, and such creatures. Holes for ventilation must be drilled in this cover. I have reared many a healthy small brood in a barrel in this way. It is easily rolled, too, into a fresh place, and if you have not coops enough, and do not know where to stow your small families, barrels or boxes must be turned to account.

The chicks when about a week old should be allowed a little liberty. The old hen might be turned out with them for an hour or so during the warm part of the day, only she must be watched in order that she does not lead them into mischief. About this time, too, their food should be changed; less soaked food and more small grain be given instead—grits, boiled barley, and other articles of diet before advised.

Chickens should never be let out too early in the morning even when they are three weeks or a month old, as it is certainly bad for them to be about while the dew is on the grass.

The coops should be constantly changed about from place to place, but never allowed to stand on wet, moist ground. One of the great secrets in rearing chickens is *always to keep them dry*. If they are allowed to be out in the wet, or kept on damp ground, they will soon become delicate. "Gapes," that fatal malady will attack them, or diarrhœa, or some other ailment, and they will soon die off.

When they begin to feather the very greatest care should be taken of them, as this is a very critical period. Hempseed and bread soaked should be given, and iron in their water. At six months they should be in full plumage, and in seven or eight months the pullets, if they have been well fed up to this time, will commence laying. "Tailings" (wheat) are really the best grain food for chickens up to four months. After they first begin to eat grain many people advise barley, but if you can get wheat—which is not, however, always easy to procure—I infinitely prefer it. If you must give barley, then let it be bruised.

I am no friend to keeping chicks indoors, as some people advise, for I am convinced it makes them weakly. Find a sheltered corner for the coop, and move them into it even in cold weather, only put the coop under shelter at night. Confining them indoors, even in a barn or a stable, appears to produce cramp and weakness of the legs, which when turned out is not the case, for the best and surest preventive for cramp and leg-weakness is to let the birds so affected have their liberty in the air, where they can get the exercise they really require.

With regard to the time for chickens to be hatched out, I rear young chickens most months in the year, but then my fowl-house is in a sheltered place and on good dry soil. If you sit late in the autumn, say in October or November, it is an advantage—that is, if you are in a fairly-sheltered, warm, dry spot—for chickens hatched in December and January bring in a handsome profit in the shape of "spring chickens." There is, of course, a good deal of risk, and immense care must be taken of the young birds during the cold weather, but if the situation is good it is well worth a trial.

By the end of June, or early in July, pullets hatched in December should, if they have been really well fed, be commencing to lay. Your early chickens will not, perhaps, be as strong as those hatched two months after, say in February and March. This is one reason why they should be reared for table. In any case I should not breed from birds hatched in the coldest winter months; but in the case of pullets, if I did not kill them all off as "spring chicks," fatten and kill them when they had finished laying, and before they began to moult; for birds hatched, say in March or April, would be really much stronger, and "selected" ones for keeping out of such broods be more to be depended on to supply the place of some of the old stock if you mean to kill any of them off.

If you wish to fatten "spring chickens" quickly for market, when they are about two months old confine them in coops and feed chiefly with moist food. In my opinion a fowl allowed its liberty has a better flavor than one confined and fed up in a coop, but it certainly does not put on flesh so quickly nor yet get so thoroughly plump and tempting-looking when trussed ready for market, therefore I should advise that those chickens fattened for sale should be kept in coops and fed up, while those for home use should be allowed their liberty until they were really wanted by the cook.

With regard to foxes, rats, and such vermin, your best safeguard against them is to house all your stock at night, and see yourself that their numbers are all right.

Rats must be waged war against. They are the greatest enemies to young ducklings, also chickens. Keep steel traps prepared, putting them down when the fowls are shut up for the night in the runs outside, and baiting them with cheese or bits of meat, only drop a little oil of rodium on the bait. In time, if you will persevere, you will either frighten them away or else catch them; but you must of course, keep your traps out of the way of the fowls themselves. Boiling coal tar poured down the holes, and followed by a deluge of water, is said to be very effectual in making rats desert a yard. I am averse to poison, because, if it is used in a fowl-house or yard, it is next to impossible to prevent an accident sooner or later. Ferreting every now and then will do good, unless your houses are adjoining barns or extensive outhouses, in which case you are more likely to lose your ferrets than destroy the vermin. The holes should be carefully stopped with a mixture of ground glass, bits of glass broken up, and ordinary plaster. Rats will not often attack glass mixed in this way. If you do use poison you must nail it up somewhere out of reach of the birds. This you can do by getting a small bit of meat, soaking it with the poison, and nailing it on to a bit of wood, nailing that again to the wall. Myself I should be afraid of the rat, in his efforts to get off the meat, dropping little bits of it on the floor, when of course the fowls would be the sufferers.

Cats are enemies also. Dogs one has not much reason to fear, but in the vicinity of a town cats of all ages and sizes will sooner or later visit you, and if there is one delicacy they prefer to another it is a young chick or duckling. They are so cunning too, it is hard to catch them.

Traps are not much good. Poisoned fish put down near where you fancy they get into the run is the only thing; but of course it must be taken away without fail before you let your fowls out of the house, and it should also be nailed to a piece of wood, which might be smeared with oil of valerian—of which some cats are so fond—to make it even more attractive. I never lost any chicks by cats, I am bound to say, and therefore should be loath to set poison down for them. I dread poison too, as I have already said, in a fowl-yard. One cat I had who took a fancy to a young duckling, but was discovered before she had eaten it, so poor ducky was tied to her neck in such a position that she could not get rid of it, and this effectually cured her of killing ducklings or chicks. A good hungry half-starved town cat, however, one could not cure by such means; it would be a case of "first catch your cat." But still cats I look on in a light of friends, unless I suffered too severely from their attacks I should not like to demolish them by such a cruel method as poison.

# FATTENING.

In feeding fowls for table, or rather for market—for I should never coop chickens to fat merely for home use, as I have before said—much depends on circumstances.

Spring chickens should be penned for fattening directly the hen shows a desire to leave them, when they are, say, five weeks old. They will not then have lost their first plump condition, and will soon, if well fed, increase rapidly in weight. They are not required to be very large; indeed, if fatted too long buyers would fancy they were not really "spring chickens," which frequently make their appearance at table not much larger than blackbirds, and are then considered all the greater delicacy.

If your chickens were hatched out in December, early in February you can put them up to fat. Their coops or cages should be placed in a warm dark sheltered place. There are a variety of different coops or pens recommended by different authorities on poultry to fat chickens. I do not remember to have seen one, however, which is, to my mind so suited to the purpose as this of which I give a description.

As far as the general conformation of the coop goes, it is made on the same plan as many others; but the adaptable shelf which is its chief feature is entirely my own idea, and if adopted would, I feel sure, give general satisfaction.

The coop itself is made of boards, sides, back, and ends of front; centre of front is barred, with the two middle bars movable. It stands on legs between two and three feet in height, the roof sloped sufficient to allow the rain to run easily off. To hold four chickens at the same time the coop should be about five feet in length, four in breadth, and three in height—that is, above the legs on which it stands. If the birds are kept in separate divisions then a little more length will have to be allowed for the partitions. This will give ample room for the birds without uncomfortably cramping them.

The bars in front of the coop should be wide enough apart to allow the birds to get their heads through easily to get at their food, which should be given them on a shelf or board. The shelf, when not in use, being fixed on hinges, would fold down in front of the coop. This is a much better plan than having a trough for food *fixed* outside, as so many coops have, the objection to it being that the food soon gets sour—I mean what is left after the birds have fed—sticking to the sides of the trough, which, if it is a box-like fixture, it is next to impossible to clean properly.

The shelf should have an upright lath nailed to it to prevent the chickens pushing the food beyond their reach in efforts to get at it, but the ledge should not be so deep as to interfere with the shelf closing against the front of the coop. Between this ledge and the coop should fit a zinc trough, the width of the division, for water.

When food is put down this water-trough should be slipped out, to be replaced when the meal is over. Two small wooden supports would prop up this miniature table; on the same plan an extra shelf is made to enlarge an ordinary table. A further use of this flat board would be to close up the front of the coop at night. It should not close entirely the barred space, room being left at the top for ventilation. Water not being required at night, the zinc trough should be removed to allow of the shelf being closed, while the wooden buttons would keep it firmly in its place, the small holes at the side of the coop supplying the extra ventilation necessary.

With regard to sanitary arrangements, before the birds are put into the coop it should be thoroughly washed with a mixture of lime and size, to destroy all vermin. This dries quite hard and does not rub off. If a *white* wash is objected to in a feeding-pen, then it could be darkened by the admixture of color, only see that there is no lead in the color mixed with the wash to procure the darker shade. The partially-boarded front will prevent the coop being too light.

The floor should be first of all of flat bars placed length-wise— fixtures these—and over them should slip in, from the back of the coop, a movable board, which should be drawn out every day and thoroughly scraped and sanded, but not washed, because if not thoroughly dry when put in the birds would get a chill, and very likely suffer from diarrhœa in consequence.

If after a meal there is any food remaining, let down the shelf and brush it off, giving it to the other fowls in order not to waste it. Food should never be allowed to remain in the sight of fattening fowls, or they will lose appetite. If they are only fed at stated times, and when they have eaten as much as they require the board is carefully cleaned and the water-trough replaced in the niche, the birds will feed again, when the time comes round for their food, with eagerness, which will not be the case if the food is left there for them to peck at.

I have had plenty of experience with fowls, having reared them for show, for eggs, and for table, and have therefore no hesitation in recommending my "adaptable shelf," as I feel certain it is an addition of the greatest use to an ordinary feeding-coop. It adds very little to the expense, is so simple that any carpenter could easily make it from a plain drawing, avoids waste of food, and insures cleanliness. As soft food is mostly used in fatting chickens, it is all the more necessary that none of it should be allowed to remain after the meal to turn sour, disagree with the birds, and take away their appetite. In a trough it is hardly possible to prevent a little lodging in the corners and sides, as if the trough is a fixture it cannot be removed to be washed; on a shelf remains of food need never be left, as the application of a hard brush for a few minutes would remove every particle, a little sand being afterwards sprinkled lightly over the board to render it perfectly sweet before the water-trough is slipped in.

Water should be constantly changed, and *boiled* water should be always used instead of that just pumped or drawn from a well or spring, as this will prevent the chickens getting diarrhœa.

You should have some plan of darkening your pens, either by letting down a tarpaulin over the top or having sliding boards to run in and out, so that the light can be regulated at will.

Some people keep their chickens separately, having their pens divided. I do not think this is really necessary if you choose

## FATTENING.                                                                 101

chickens of the same brood to fat together. Four are enough to fat at a time; but never allow your coop, if you have only one, to remain empty; as you kill off one lot of chickens you should have another batch ready to put in. Cramming I am entirely averse to. It is a needlessly cruel and disgusting custom, though very frequently practiced, especially in France.

Now comes the grand question of food. It should always be pultaceous; the birds cannot pick up pebbles and little stones when shut up, so cannot, digest grain of any sort. Feed them on bread and milk, oatmeal and milk, rice well boiled with a little pepper mixed with it, barley-meal, Indian corn meal, potatoes steamed and mixed with barley-meal, chopped green food, &c. Very many breeders give a large amount of suet mixed with the food, but unless people are fond of greasy fat on their poultry, which to me is an abomination, I should not advise it, as it makes the flesh so gross. *Vary the diet as much as possible*, and never give it in a sloppy state, but crumbly. Three weeks or a month at the outside is enough to keep fowls up for fatting: if kept longer the confinement begins to tell on them. Some people mix treacle or sugar with their food. Saccharine matter is no doubt conducive to fat, and oatmeal, or Indian corn ground into meal and mixed with treacle until it is in a crumbling state, is a food all chickens are fond of, but should only be given to those you wish to feed; it would not do for those pullets you wish to bring on to lay quickly, as it would develop interior fat, which is always fatal to constant laying.

Guard against waste of food. Only experience will cause you to know how much to supply at once; and until you learn this, directly you see the chickens begin to pick daintily at their food remove it, give to the other fowls then what is left, but on no account allow it to stay in the trough for the fatting chickens to eat, when, as the old women say, "they've a mind to." If they do not constantly see food before them they will eat it far more readily when it is given. This is only common-sense treatment, and, believe me, in dealing with fowls you must often draw largely on this very desirable commodity.

Four meals a day should be the allowance for penned-up chickens, letting them eat, each time you feed, as much as they will with appetite. At night they will roost on the board. Some people put down clean straw, but if you close up the pen so that the birds are not cold it is not really necessary, and it only harbours insects. Perches you might have if you've room in your pen—sufficient height I mean. Before the birds are put in have the coop well cleaned, white-washed, and sprinkled with carbolic acid. This should be done two or three times during the time the chicks are fattening.

Fowls should of course be killed in the most merciful way. It makes one shudder to read of the manner in which the poor things are sometimes tortured, allowed to bleed slowly to death, pins run into their brains, and horrors too dreadful to name. Poultry dealers generally kill them in the quickest manner by breaking their necks, and so quickly do they perform their work that one man will often kill and pick a dozen or more in an hour. One of the easiest ways of killing is to hit the bird a sharp blow on the back of the head with a heavy blunt stick; death is almost instantaneous. Then pluck at once while the bird is warm, as the process can then be accomplished much more rapidly than if the bird is allowed to hang until cold. When all the feathers are off the fowl will still be warm. It should then be carefully singed, floured, and trussed, and placed between two boards with a weight, on the topmost; not too heavy a weight, of course, to spoil its shape, but just enough to keep the breast down and in good shape.

Capons of course fetch much better prices, and their flesh remains tender up to the age of two years, whereas a cock at that age is only eatable in a stew, or pie. Chickens converted into capons increase in size to a wonderful extent; the birds will in a year be nearly treble the size it would have been if left alone, and double the market value.

In conclusion I may observe that I can most sincerely, from my own practical experience, advise all ladies, as well as gentlemen, who have a little room to spare in their back gardens, to set up poultry-keeping on a small scale. Many more people keep fowls now than used to years ago, I know, but still not half people enough. Many who have room to spare for a family of fowls let that room remain unoccupied, either from a mistaken idea that poultry-keeping is too expensive or will entail too much trouble on them. With regard to the latter idea, it is, no doubt, a partially true one. Fowls do cause trouble, and if they are to be made to pay their way cannot fail to do so. But whatever trouble they cause they are worth it, and no undertaking or pursuit that I ever heard of flourished without some amount of trouble. In return they give fresh eggs—that you are sure of, and can offer a guest without any inward misgivings—plump chickens, a little pocket-money, and a great deal of interest.

www.ingramcontent.com/pod-product-compliance
Lightning Source LLC
Chambersburg PA
CBHW020158170426
43199CB00010B/1101